HOW TO G
DREAM SCHOOL WITHOUT
LYING, BRIBING OR
PHOTOSHOPPING

"Insider secrets" of how to 10X your odds of admission, legally and ethically

For the Kersch Family :)

Andy Lockwood

ANDY LOCKWOOD

www.LockwoodCollegePrep.com

First Comments and Bonus

Understatement of the Century: the college admissions landscape has changed a wee bit this year (AHEM, Felicity, Lori!).

Yet, it hasn't really changed that much.

I think a more accurate way of describing the college scandal is that it shed light on the craziness that goes on, behind the scenes.

Yes, Rick Singer and his clients and co-conspirators crossed a line (Understatement of the Century II), but, there could be some good that emerges from this mess.

First, assuming you're not as nuts as the ones indicted and yet-to-be-indicted in this scheme, NOW you finally know exactly what - and whom - you and your kids are competing against: parents willing to do almost anything to give their kids an edge. Now you know, and realize that you can't put your head in the sand any longer, hoping things will "work out" by themselves.

Second, it's my belief that the College Board and the ACT will make it harder for children to receive accommodations such as extra time or untimed exams. I had been chirping about this problem before the scandal broke, then some enterprising reporters wrote up stories about how in affluent areas such as Scarsdale, NY and Newton, MA[1], one-in-five and one-in-three students received accommodations, compared to 1.6% of students in low-income areas (*Many More Students, Especially the Affluent, Get Extra Time to Take the SAT, Wall Street Journal, May 21, 2019*).

Unfortunately, this will likely mean that kids who truly deserve extra time will now have to jump through more hoops to get them. My advice is to explore accommodations long before 11th grade, so you do not get accused of having STOD (Standardized Testing

---

[1] They cited my high school, Newton North. Tiger Pride!

Development Disorder[2]).   On the one hand, tighter rules will cut down on the number of kids gaming the system, in theory.

On the other hand, I'm afraid that new procedures will throw the baby out with the bath water, by denying otherwise deserving children the accommodations they deserve.   If you suspect your child learns differently, explore with your high school a 504 or an IEP (Individualized Education Plan) in 9th or 10th grade, at the latest.

This book is designed to help you and your children successfully navigate today's post-Felicity college admissions landscape. Hopefully you find some common sense, practical and tactical advice that will remove some stress and help your kiddos get into their top choice colleges.

If you'd like to go "deeper" than the pages in this book, I recommend that you sign up for our free webinar, *The Dirty Little Secrets of What It REALLY Takes to Get Into a Top College Today:*

Go to www.CollegeAdmissionsWebcast.com for the rest of the story.

---

[2] I made that term up, but you have to admit it's catchy, right?

TABLE OF CONTENTS

DEDICATION

This book is for stressed out parents and teens who are overwhelmed by the college process, and underwhelmed by traditional, mainstream advice that they may be getting from their guidance counselors.

If this sounds like you, and/or you are confused or upset by any of the following thoughts or questions:

- You have no idea whether your kid will be able to get into a decent school

- You're not sure what a "decent" school is, especially because they all seem the same

- Kids apply to a universe of 30 or so colleges out of the almost 4,000 choices, you're wondering why…

- You think there has to be a more meaningful way to pick colleges other than looking at rear window stickers of cars in your neighborhood or confining your list to the colleges playing football or basketball on TV

- Your kid has no idea what he wants to major in or where he should go

- You have serious doubts if your kid will learning ANYTHING useful in college and you don't want to pay $250,000 for him to goof around or "find himself"

- You feel "behind" - some parents act like their kids have already gotten into Yale by 8th grade and desperately want you to know about it

I'm writing this book to tell you a little bit about how we approach college planning, which I hope will help you get to know us and decide whether to pursue a college consulting relationship with us some day. However, a warning: this book - and our approach - is NOT for everybody.

For example, this book is not for parents who blame teachers or coaches when their kids get a bad grade or do not get enough playing time. If you are generally perceived as a blamey, complainy[3] sort of person (ask your friends if you can't tell), you should not read any further.

Also, this book is NOT for parents who think it's helpful to do the applications or essays for their kids, not to mention bribe a proctor or sailing coach. (The truth: this is actually a disservice.)

And it's not for kids who want parents to do the applications or essays for them, either.

Last, this book is not for parents or kids who believe that any college OWES them an acceptance.

But if you want the best for your child, meaning that you see college as a means to a successful end: a satisfying career that allows your grown up child to have the income and lifestyle he or she desires...

...as opposed to a top priority of pasting the name of highly-ranked college on the rear window of your car..

...then this book is for you!

---

[3] Should be a word.

PROLOGUE

THOUGHTS ON THE COLLEGE ADMISSIONS SCANDAL

Andy on Cavuto Coast to Coast, not looking particularly outraged

I'm writing this in May 2019, after discussing the Felicity Huffman/Lori Louglin/Rick Singer college admissions scandal approximately 5,487 times. If you're wondering what my thoughts are, have no fear, I've devoted the first few chapters of this book to that, but...

...only inasmuch as they pertain to you - a parent of a college-bound teen.

Below is the unedited version of an opinion piece that was published in Newsday March 13, 2019.

I am a private college advisor, and have a slightly different take on the recent college admissions scandal.

I'm disgusted by the lack of fairness described by the indictment, and on behalf of the hard working kids who didn't get in because their spots were "taken" by rich kids of scummy clients of William "Rick" Singer.

But the only shocking thing is that people are shocked! "Pay to play" exists in all walks of life, such as government contracts to operate restaurants, jobs for donors to political campaigns and, more recently college admissions.

Colleges are businesses and have their own institutional agendas, such as recruiting kids from underprivileged economic backgrounds, underrepresented minorities, legacies and recruited athletes.

Oh, and "Development" cases, i.e. ultra wealthy families who the administration hopes will donate to the college's endowment. Businesses need money to cover their expenses and grow. Not a newsflash that admissions isn't a pure meritocracy.

However, I readily admit that I was surprised by some aspects of this scandal, but perhaps not how you might think.

I actually met "Rick" Singer in 2010. A mutual friend introduced and warned me that he believed only approximately 80% of the words that came out of Singer's mouth.

So my old partner and I met Singer in a nondescript office in Miami, where he proceeded to tell me about his business, how Tony Robbins sold him the name for his business ("The Edge") and how he flew all over to meet clients such as Steve Jobs.

"There's the 20%!" I thought.

But that wasn't what I had the hardest time with. Singer told me that an Arab Sheik contacted him, because his son was waitlisted at Georgetown University. He heard that Singer had a "side door" way of getting him in.

The Sheik, by way of Singer, offered Georgetown $6M to pry him loose. (I shudder to think what the "back door" was!)

Here's the part I had the toughest time swallowing: according to Singer, Georgetown said no!

My first thoughts were, "Good for them!" because I suspected that this was the exception, not the rule.

My next thought was, "Why would a Sheik care where his kid went to college?"

Singer's answer was one word: status. Being in the right social circles.

I found myself wondering the same thing when this story broke. I understand, on some level, that private equity guys, CEOs and celebrities crave status. We all do, on some level.

So I see the argument for Stanford, Yale and other similar schools. But UCLA? The University of San Diego (acceptance rate: 50%)?

No offense, but has the obsession with college status filtered down to "Second Tier" and lower schools?

The bigger question is, what does all of this mean for "normal" families with college-bound teens? Here's what I'm telling clients and parents at my workshops and webinars:

Yes, the "system" is rigged.

Yes, I wish things were different.

But they're not. It's not helpful to live in the "Land of Shoulds," to quote my wife, Pearl.

Instead, I prefer to deal with how things are on Planet Earth. Reality.

Some stuff is out of your control, some is entirely within your control.

You can't change who your parents are, their bank accounts or where they went to college or what TV show they appeared on.

But you CAN affect your academic performance, the courses you take, your standardized test scores and extracurricular activities.

You can also choose the colleges you apply to. If you don't get into an elite college, the world will continue to spin on its axis.

There is zero proven correlation between where someone goes to college and how much they earn. (Google "Dale and Krueger").

Our kids will be successful during their four years of college, and, more importantly, the 40-plus post-college years, based on their *efforts*, not where they went to college: their work ethic, grit and resilience.

Qualities that money and wire fraud cannot buy.

CHAPTER 1

PREDICTIONS FOR OUR POST-FELICITY WORLD

A couple of weeks after "L'affaire Lori" broke, a mom asked me if I thought there would be any changes, now that we're living in a post Felicity-Lori world.

My answer was two-fold.

First, I posited that I don't think we've hit POST-scandal status. I suspect that many of the parents accused of these High College Crimes and Misdemeanors will "give up" some of their friends and even family in order to curry favor with the FBI and reduce their own sentences.

In terms of stuff that could affect YOU, i.e. your 10th or 11th grader, or younger, I have a few deep thoughts to discuss.

Unfortunately, I think it will be harder to obtain extended time accommodations for SAT and ACT testing. I say "unfortunately" because I'm fearful that new rules could throw the baby out with the bathwater, i.e make it harder on the kids who really deserve accommodations to get them.

The others, who don't really need it although they suffer from STOD (Standardized Test Onset Disorder), SHOULD have a harder time getting extra time for the tests when they didn't show any signs of learning issues in 9th and 10th grades.

(To anticipate your next question, yes, I made up STOD.)

I conducted my own non-scientific poll over the last few weeks, asking practically every student I encountered whether they knew of other kids in their high school who got extra time, but didn't need it. Approximately 100% said yes.

On to prediction #2. Don't be surprised if high school administrators attempt to burden guidance counselors with the duty of verifying what kids put on their college applications.

Previously, we've operated under the honor system, but I've already started to hear rumblings that counselors will need to take more of an active role to determine whether the robotics team had 17 co-founders, or young Robert really put in 347 hours of community service in 11th grade.

I don't know how far this will go, because guidance counselors are already overburdened (the ratio of kids to counselor is 400:1 in New York, closer to 500:1 nationally and most guidance counselors report that they spend only 20% of their time on college-related activities). Maybe all I'm hearing is lip service that won't amount to anything, maybe it's more.

Advice

If you suspect that your child needs accommodations, don't wait - take care of this immediately - these things take time to approve. Get thyself to an educational psychologist immediately, tarry not.

If you have a 10th grader, start your prep early and often. Summer before 11th is ideal, even if your kiddo isn't "ready." The more reps you get in, the better you'll do, it's that simple.

(If you're local to Long Island or interested in Skype tutoring, See our test prep site, www.LockwoodTestPrep.com.)

Bit of Advice No 3: Be prepared to have EVERYTHING verified on your college applications, possibly by your guidance counselor, possibly by your admissions officer. Or maybe by a third party contracted out to double-check the veracity of your applications, who knows?

CHAPTER 2

LOCKWOOD LATEST COLLEGE ADVISOR ENSNARED BY SCANDAL

[This was originally published as a blog post April 1, 2019]

Boston, Massachusetts:

FBI agent John McGillicuddy III announced today that the FBI had indicted another college advisor, Andy Lockwood, as part of its widening college admissions probe.

"According to our key witness, Ms. Avrille Furst, Lockwood first approached Furst back on April 1, 2018, promising her and her daughter, Avril Furst the 2nd, a 'side door' into any college with a 50% or worse admittance rate."

Ms. Furst and Ms. Furst the 2nd rebuffed Lockwood, according to testimony, at which time Lockwood then promised an "underground, tunneled door" into any college a 50% of worse admittance rate, and explained his scheme.

According to testimony, the scheme allegedly involved Lockwood contacting the Quidditch and Ultimate Frisbee coaches at up to seven colleges, photoshopping Ms. Furst the 2nd's face into a Quidditch uniform (which was not easy, according to Lockwood, as it required a high degree of skill, because of the cape) and bribe the schools' coaches with offers of up to $478, in small, unmarked bills.

When the Fursts protested that Avril Furst didn't know how to play Quidditch, Lockwood - recorded via wire tap - responded, "Don't worry about it, I've got it rigged. Just watch the first three Harry Potter movies again."

Another parent, Averell Fuhl, parent of a high school senior and scion of the Fuhl asbestos fortune, testified that Lockwood promised his son "the sun, moon and a law degree from Thomas Cooley School of Law," even though Fuhl's son was a middling student at a prep school in New England, and only in 12th grade.

"Hey, if Cooley's good enough for Trump's old lawyer Cohen, it's damn well good enough for you. Just give me 10 minutes and I'll print you up that degree," Lockwood bragged, which was also recorded.

"And I won't need to go the Quidditch route on this one - as long as you can fog a mirror and write a check, you're golden! " Lockwood added, according to sealed court documents.

When reached for comment, Lockwood asked, "Are you guys from Fox?" When told no, he then refused to comment, instead referring reporters to his attorney, Michael Avenatti.

Lockwood is scheduled to be arraigned April 31.

CHAPTER 3

INTERVIEW ON COLLEGE SCANDAL WITH DON BETTERTON, FORMER ADMISSIONS COMMITTEE MEMBER, PRINCETON UNIVERSITY

[Note: I am extremely lucky to have Don Betterton as a business partner and mentor, who served on the admissions committee and as director of financial aid for 30 years at Princeton University. And you are fortunate as well, because this lightly edited transcript of an interview for my podcast, *The College Planning Edge*, contains unique, "Burning Bush" insight from a true insider that you simply cannot find anywhere else.

Andy: Alright Andy Lockwood here, welcome to a special edition of the *College Planning Edge* podcast. Unless you've been living under a rock, you've heard about the college scandal involving bribes and lying and photoshopping and wiretapping. I reached out to a friend and mentor of mine who graciously agreed to let me bring him on this podcast, Mr Don Betterton. Hello Mr Betterton.

Don: Hi Andy how you doing?

Andy: So let's just get right into it, what's your take on this whole thing involving Rick Singer, the college admissions advisor who's now under indictment.

Don: Yeah my first take is I'm surprised of how much of a widespread news item it is. I think when it started, this was about a week ago, and literally for at least two or three days the newspapers the headlines on the TV news, whatever happened to be discussions among people seem to be centered on this to a great extent at the exclusion of you know we've got a few issues going on in the world. So the fact that it seemed to hit the central nervous system of so many for whatever reason took out of it, I really was rather surprised, I think that the Hollywood connection probably kicked it off, but it did sustain itself longer and the more serious way than I thought it would.

Andy: Now I don't want to put words in your mouth, but I had a very similar reaction, were you surprised because this is just one of these things that everyone kind of knows happens, or some other reason?

Don: Yeah. I don't know what people thought, I think they kind of had the idea that getting into college was a merit-based thing, but they also realize there were athletes, there was affirmative action programs, there was some other ways to do things. But I what this is it kind of get behind the curtain, and really show in detail how these, what these different areas were and I guess in particular how they can me manipulated in an unfair way. I think that's what really, the unfairness of it is what I think got to people.

Andy: Yeah, I think so and like you said, there's this sort of hope that it's a meritocracy, but that's just not the way things work in reality I guess is that fair to say speaking behind the curtain in the admissions committee?

Don: Yeah exactly, I think it's been well known that there are spots for athletes and there is a what we call a "development list." There's a list that goes up with either past donors or potential donors it goes on. There's obviously the SAT's very important, the higher the SAT

12

the better the chance of admissions. And there's things like that, so I think maybe, it's almost like a conspiracy theory, those people always thought there was more going on than they thought, now, "Aha! It really is like that," these colleges aren't as sanctimonious and straight as they thought. So maybe this was kind of a "gotcha" aspect to it as well. I don't know what's on their minds, but I just thought that, there was an awful lot of people who were very interested and had a strong opinion, more than I thought there would be.

Andy: Yeah I've been saying that the only thing shocking to me was that people were actually shocked.

Don: Yeah right. Yep I agree with that.

Andy: So tell me about, if you can, how much does it really matter, or was does it take to buy your way into an exclusive school. Does that actually happen? Is there a certain dollar amount, is there a certain building that you have to put up, what's the story?

Don: Yeah I think the generally accepted understanding is that colleges need money to operate all the things they do...by the way including financial aid programs that gives the money back to the poor students - let's not forget that there's a big commitment for poor disadvantaged students, while we're looking at this rich end of things, there's also a very strong commitment on the poor end.

Don: And there's a procedure, there's what's called either Development or the Advancement office at a university, and they raise money from alums, from corporations, from foundations, whatever happens to be. And particularly when doing alums or the friends of the university, the office hears somewhere along the way that possibly the child's coming along will be an applicant. And there's this discussion takes place between the development rep and the parents. And they talk a bit back and forth. The easiest case is if the parents have given a good deal of money for a long period of time, then that student will almost automatically go on a development list and will eventually be forwarded to admissions.

Don: On the other hand, there might be money that has not yet been given, from as a pledge or not, but there's an indication that the family will be generous if the student is admitted.

Don: At Princeton we call it a "tag:" there's an athletic tag, there's a minority tag, there's a legacy tag, whatever it happens to be. There's various categories that get a little extra bonus in admissions, and one of it is the development group, and they send a list to the admissions, obviously much like the coach would, much like the music professor would to look for musicians or whatever. So there's always different groups around university looking for particular people that they support, will try and list to admissions, please take an extra look beyond whatever the SAT GPA, whatever it is, we'd like to have this student for whatever reason, on our campus.

Don: And there's a good deal of that, not to digress too much but generally when you're talking about competitive colleges, there's three levels of admissions. One, would be the very best kids, there's no question they admit them. Then the next level is the tags, people who get a bonus, special consideration for whatever reason, and they take that group, that's the second level. And the third level would be all those other who are left over who aren't extremely talented all the way round at the top academically, otherwise who doesn't have any of this tag attached to them, and that's the group more or less your regular smart bright kids.

Don: And what makes college so competitive, I know I'm digressing a bit here, is often times when your pool is so large and your admit rate is so small, once you've taken the very best, and you've taken all those tag kids, there's really not many spots left over for the really good solid kid that seems like he should be admitted but there's simply no room for him.

Don: That's digressing a little bit but that's kind of the way it works.

Andy: Yeah none of that is a digression cause it's just so interesting, I'm furiously scribbling notes here.

Andy: I remember I read a book once by a former admissions officer I believe at Duke University **[Note: *Admissions Confidential* by Rachel Toor]** who estimated that anywhere from two thirds to up to 80 percent of the slots at any given competitive college are reserved for these tags, or these special categories, does that sound or feel right to you?

Don: I think that's quite high. It depends how he counts that. If you say engineers for an example might be a group or artists or whatever so I don't think it's a categorization but I don't think they get a particular big admissions break. But I think the two big ones I think would be, the athletes I think in most cases are probably the largest group, depending upon the schools legacies probably come next. Then it depends how you look at the affirmative action categories, I think you can call that a tag, so I think depending upon the commitment to minorities and disadvantaged and overcoming obstacles, and first generation college and all that kind of thing, that's probably the largest group, if you want

15

to call that a tag. And then miscellaneous categories including development cases.

Don: But I would say all of them probably don't add up to more than 30 or maybe 40 percent. Did you say up to 80 percent is that the number you quoted?

Andy: Yeah. I was from this book, I think the author was named Rachel Toor, and she estimated two thirds, and some people think as high as 80 percent.

Don: Well she would have to include a lot of categories that I wouldn't include. She probably included engineers maybe geographic diversity, maybe international students, so she's probably quoted a lot of other categories beyond the ones I would list.

Andy: Yes I think she did include international and other sort of special categories that met institutional goals, above and beyond just pure academic considerations, you know grades, and SAT and ACT.

Don: Yeah but see in those cases some of those students don't need a break at all, they tend to be very strong anyway. International students are a very strong group, so it's not as if you would reach deep into that pool like you might for a development case or an athlete, so I would classify those differently.

Andy: Okay. So circling back to the donor in the development cases, you made a very interesting point which I just read about this morning in an article in the *Wall Street Journal*, a counterpoint on should college be a pure meritocracy versus this is the way it works. The argument was that a lot of the money that gets donated from the development types of cases, goes toward funding financial aid for low income families. I think the statistic was 49 percent, quoted by the president of the National Association of Financial Aid

Administrators. So I find that very interesting. You mentioned that a lot of that money from the development cases goes toward financial aid, do you think that's a fair estimate?

Don: Oh yeah I very much agree with that. I think that's one of the most common reason that alums, Independent or dependent of where their children are in high school, give money for, it's very very popular. A lot of it's kind of unrestricted, so most the unrestricted money goes right back into financial aid. And then for restricted money, at least at Princeton, the most commonly was to establish a scholarship, and the endowment just continues on over time, and the income from that each year gives individual students scholarships. And then I think in addition to that you might get some grants to academic departments for programs, and every now and then a building, something like that, but I certainly agree that financial aid would be the highest percent of where the money goes that's given to the university.

Andy: So when you say restricted, just to clarify, that means that the donor says "I'm giving you this money but I need you to use it for X, Y and Z?"

Don: Yeah that's right. There's what's called general funds, you just give it to the university, no strings attached, normally what's called annual giving the money that alums give each year is unrestricted. When they give their donation they can check I'd like it to go to student aid, I'd like it to go here or there, but for the most part, the university can use it any way they want. Then some of these other cases, like one of these development case, they maybe talking about a building, or a residential college, and they're looking for money specifically for that purpose, and normally the name of the donor then is attached to that gift. The residential college at Princeton is the Whitman Residential College, which was from Meg Whitman, who used to be Ebay and then Hewlett Packard and whatever. Or maybe a program in a department, for Chinese history or something like that. So they can have name gifts usually attached to a restriction, or you can have what's called general funds, can be used for anything, in that case it's mostly for student aid.

Andy: Okay and I want to circle back to another comment you made when you were describing the whole process of admission. So the people who are on this development list, it didn't sound like that they're just rubber stamped and admitted to the university?

Don: Right, they aren't. Similar to the athletic list, to delve in both areas, and typically let's say a list goes up of 10 soccer players, or 10 development cases. And then what happens is the list is ordered in a way that either the coach or the development officer would like to see the students admitted. However the admissions office makes the final decision. So in the case of the soccer list, they number one guy maybe turned down and the number two will be taken because the SAT is stronger or GPA is stronger. So the list is there, but the admissions office has the right, the priority, the responsibility to take in an order that's best for the university as a whole. And the same thing happens with development, they may turn down that one who has the chance to give the largest gift, and take number four or five, the gift is maybe more modest but the student is simply better, they'd rather have that student there.

Don: So admissions always has the final say, which kind of gets back to this guy (Rick Singer) and the guarantee, I don't know how he can completely guarantee anything, he probably has a pretty good idea maybe at the 90 percent level whether this'll go through but still admissions people have the authority and the right to

18

make the final decision. No matter what list they're on, no matter what the numbers are involved.

Andy: Yeah I definitely want to get to that too, but I want to ask you about the duty of an admissions person or whoever's at the next level after the coach, like in this case with Singer. He would pay off a coach allegedly, who would then put a kid on the tennis team list even though the guy hadn't played tennis since 9th grade, and say this is one of the people that we want. After that, Is there any duty of oversight, and do you think this is going to change if there isn't? Should the athletic liaison to the admissions department to say, wait a minute, how come this kid hasn't played on a team since 9th grade?

Don: Well they had to pay off the coaches basically because they can't just rig the athletic profile, which consists of the all star teams they played on, and this and that. Because the coach is going to interview the student, or he knows the athlete's coaching references, so the coach would soon find out this is a fake athlete. So that's why (Singer) had the family actually give the money to the coaches. So then the coach presents the kid to admissions, but it looks like Singer and his group made the credentials strong enough so when the coach finally put this kid number one or number two, whatever, on the list, they really knew that a student with those credentials, and this place on my list is going to be admitted. So once again I know that's not 100 percent, but probably get to be pretty high.

Don: What usually happens in the athletic department is that all the coaches list go through an athletic department assistant associate director, who's the admission liaison. So those are the two who talk about these lists. How strong are they, what teams need what, which student are we going to admit. So those are the two key people

19

involved, the athletic department liaison and the admissions liaison.

Don: So in the case of I think it was USC, they had paid that athletic department liaison a considerable amount of money to make this thing go. So in that case either the coaches or that individual were definitely involved. Just to present the athletes, even fake or whatever, would not work without inside support.

Andy: So the Yale soccer coach allegations where he took $450,000 or something, isn't there a red flag that if a kid gets presented to admissions and then drops or never plays a game or never shows up for practice, assuming it happened more than once?

Don: Well no admissions wouldn't notice that, they admit the tennis player and they get on with the next year's class. They don't know whether that tennis player ever shows up for the team, or plays for a year and drops out, they would not know. I don't know if any of these things and these students were scholarship athletes, I'm not sure any of the were. In that case if they've got a scholarship, and they tend to drop out, maybe the word gets known if it's more of a more major sport of whatever. But no I don't think admissions would track at all whether these students stay with the sport of even go out initially. I don't think they'd know that.

Andy: I think the sailing coach at Stanford offered a "Books Scholarship," like $1500, to one of his recruits. I don't think there's any other scholarships involved besides a $1000 or nominal amount.

Don: Yeah it's probably not relevant, certainly I didn't know whether there's full scholarships or not, maybe only has book scholarships I'm not sure how that would work. It's not a major sport so I wouldn't assume he has much in the way of money so maybe that's what he has for everybody.

Andy: I didn't even know it (Sailing) was an NCAA sport, I figured it was a club.

Don: I don't think it is, I don't think it is a NCAA sport, maybe it's like equestrian something like that where it comes under some other organization, could very well be.

Andy: I'm starting a Quidditch recruiting scheme and looking at Ultimate Frisbee.

Don: (Ignoring.) The other thing is, I wonder is what the transcript looked like in the teachers recommendations and all that. I haven't heard at all about that. I assume that if there was anything like that, the high school counselor would have blown the whistle earlier, I *really haven't done anything for this student and I didn't see the application go in, the transcript wasn't strong*, so I'm kind of curious whether in these cases, the transcript and the recommendation, everything that we haven't talked about, was strong enough to be admitted. So I'm kind of curious about that, whether they (Singer) actually arranged for a transcript as well or whether they just assumed the student was strong enough and the athletic tag or raising the SAT's was enough, I don't know, I've always had that question, haven't seen anything about it written. I know occasionally I think a guidance counselor wondered why the student got in here or there.

Andy: Yeah, that's interesting, I hadn't thought of that. That can't be so easy to do because most of these counselors use Naviance (to upload transcripts) and everything's uploaded electronically and the Common App, right?

Don: And certainly if Singer's group did this, then somewhere along the way a counselor would say "Well, how did you get in, I don't think I filled out the school report or sent a transcript," so I guess they relied on the legitimate transcript and teachers recs. But I would have expected that would have kicked a couple kids out, that's why the 100 percent guarantee, I just question how that would be possible. And in the Yale case, the Ivy's have a academic index that they use where it's SAT's and GPA and a bunch of other things, and that student no matter what, would have to get over that level **[Note: to prevent Ivy League schools from recruiting "ringers," the colleges adopted an Academic Index, which mandates that each team has a minimum average GPA, class rank SAT/ACT etc]**. So even if there might have been extra push, if the student did get into Yale through this, he or she had to be pretty, well in this case women's soccer, she had to really be pretty good (academically) to start with, so the main thing I guess was getting on the list for that little extra advantage of being on the list would do.

Andy: Yeah, well that's probably one of the driving forces between having the 1440 or whatever the magic number was - the tutor (Mark Riddell) who was paid off had to hit that on behalf of the recruited athlete in order to adhere to that academic index.

Don: Yeah if it really was that sophisticated and knew what the academic index numbers were and made sure that SAT was high enough to get over that threshold, that would do it, you're right. Maybe he (Singer) knows what the formula is and maybe made sure that the student met the standards, that could be.

Andy: I was actually talking to a client of mine who's daughter was tutored legitimately by (Riddell, when at IMG, the tennis and other sports academy in Florida), my understanding of how he became susceptible was because he was being paid $65 an hour by IMG, even though he's a Harvard grad and he really needed money because he was having a baby. But I guess my question to you is, how easy is it for this to happen, despite the College Board's recent changes in terms or requiring picture ID, somehow Singer was still able to find special proctors and proctoring centers. How does that happen?

Don: Yeah that was interesting, once again this guy found, let's say the weak spots and the holes in the system, because if they (Singer's clients) would have just sat in a regular test taking, and for whatever reason they had a way of cheating and they're copying from the person next to them of whatever, the College Board has a very sophisticated algorithms to catch what was called normal cheating, and they would cancel the score and ask the kid to take again whatever.

Don: So he really was clever in setting up a special center, looks like there was one proctor there, it was accommodation kids, some kind of learning difference, and apparently he paid off the proctor at that center, and it could have been these kids only went there, that was solely for the purpose of those kids, one or two or three at a time I don't know. And so then he somehow he had this other person take the test, or when the test were handed in they changed the answers or something, so that kinda stayed outside all the College Board checking systems.

Don: I haven't read much about ACT, but I assume they do things the same way. So that was a really clever way to get around a very sophisticated way the College Board has in place to catch what I would call normal cheaters. And that was an elaborate set up as you know: firstly, the kids had to get extra time so they didn't take it at the

23

regular test center where the school was, not even take it at the special time accommodation at their school, there's usually 100 kids in a room taking the test regular, then there's two or three kids with some type of accommodation taking it in another room another day or even on two days. So he got his kids sent off to another place where he paid the proctor, and that's where this thing took place.

Don: So once again it's a little bit like what he says the side door, he avoided the development where it was a lot of money and no guarantee, and he moved that away to another one ("door") and he also took the SAT thing (cheating) where they were liable to be caught and moved that to another venue, so it's kind of interesting, in a sick way.

Don: Very clever, and of course he was so clever he probably thought he wouldn't be caught, but that part didn't work.

Andy: It's so elaborate and I told you offline that I had met him back in 2009 before these alleged things started to happen - who knows. He actually told me that he specialized in using the "side door," which he explained to me at the time meant parents donating $250,000, not multi millions of dollars. But we never talked of any of these elaborate schemes, so when I learned about them, they kind of blew me away.

Andy: So just let me segway into something that is not just purely a Rick Singer thing, but when you mention accommodations, that was another one of these things where, there was a lot of moral outrage, for people who were gaming the system. I read over the weekend an article that I think between 2006 and 2011 or so, the number of people requesting accommodations to the College Board doubled. And that's one of these worst kept secrets that I see in my practice. There's been a huge uptake in people requesting accommodations: they get their kids an advantage, kids who's otherwise shown no form of learning differences or disabilities, who somehow qualify for extra time on the SAT or ACT. What's your take on that, how easy is it to get accommodations, and have you noticed the same thing?

Don: Actually it's pretty hard, that's another thing I have question about, and I would say for both ACT and SAT, they're very similar rules as to how to do this, now as far as I know in almost all cases the student already has to have accommodation in high school, which takes going to a psychologist and getting all this kind of evaluations and things and the high school then approves the extra time in the high school or whatever the different type of accommodation happens to be, use a computer or whatever, and then it becomes a relatively easy for the ACT or SAT to say okay you've already been approved, we trust that. Send the paperwork where you got the accommodation in high school, and we'll approve it for this, SAT or ACT. As far as I know that is the standard procedure almost all the way along.

Don: So did he lead this thing so much that he got these kid two or three years ahead of time, accommodated in high school, so they would then move and get accommodated for the SAT and ACT. I guess he did, I can't imagine them suddenly get accommodation just like that, it's a fairly long detailed process to do, do he may have very well started early and made sure they got it in school, but then again I get back to, what is this school observing in this, if the student was in these accommodation situations in high school, the counselor must have known about it, he or she must have looked at the paperwork. If not all of a sudden a student gets accommodation, the counsel would wonder why the student's getting extra time to go in another test center.

Don: I don't know I have some questions kind of behind the scenes of how some of this really happened. I just scratch my head a little bit over of it.

Andy: Yeah I was just literally going to say that I'm scratching my head too. I think that same article, I believe in *The New York Times*, written by a psychologist, estimated that the College Board approves 85 percent of the extra time and other accommodations, so maybe it's hard to do unless you have some kind of very friendly, or on the payroll psychologist who is allowing this to happen, or rubber stamping the application.

Andy: My wife Pearl has a friend who lives in another state, whose son goes to a private high school. She said that he takes the test timed, and there's four other kids in the room - everyone else is taking it with accommodations!

Don: They sometimes even take it over a couple days I guess, I think somebody who did the ACT took two of the tests on one day and two of them the next day. So once again it's (the accommodations) there for good legitimate reasons, which some of these groups are worried about now, they're going to crack down on it, which will hurt the legitimate kids, so we'll see what happens. The are careful procedures in place, and somehow he (Singer) found a way to take advantage of. So it's another thing he thought through and was able to make it happen. But it wouldn't have happened if he hadn't set up the special test center with the proctor that he paid off and maybe the guy who was, the test expert might even been on site changing answers I'm not sure.

Don: He had to not only know things at the first level which might not of worked, he had to even go to the next level to make sure he did all the things to be successful, he certainly put a lot of time and effort in on this. We don't want to use the word "admiration" for the guy, he sure worked hard to understand the system, how to get around it and he paid an awful lot of money to get around it.

Andy: Just imagine if he stayed legitimate - how great an advisor he could be!

Don: You would think that right, a guy that bright, knows so much, he probably just had a regular practice, he could have charged let's say the going rate nowadays is 5 - 10 thousand dollars, he could have charged 20,000 or maybe a little bit more for the wealthy families, say "I'm not guaranteeing anything," and send them off to whatever the appropriate school was, and I think the parents would be satisfied in most cases.

Don: There's this mania, the prestige mania for how much more the parents will pay to put Yale in the back of their car instead of Penn State, that's the driving force behind this whole thing. And they don't have to be the wealthiest people in Hollywood or in business, it's just pervasive in our society. I see it all the time and I deal with more or less middle income families, but the value of that prestige, on that end drives what this guy was able to do on the other end right.

Andy: So I see that too, but then I remember when the story came out, I was looking at the schools that were involved, and it's not just Yale and Stanford, it's the University of San Diego which admits 50 percent, and it's USC and...

Don: Yeah that surprised me, that's a solid school and Wake Forest is in that category, little bit stronger, but yeah it wasn't just Harvard or Princeton. USC is kinda up there,

27

I think there may have been more of a local prestige for the Hollywood set, but yeah the fact that there was some other. University of Texas Austin, I've had some pretty, I wouldn't call them normal kids, I'd call average good kids get in UT Austin, they don't have to be off the charts good. And Wake Forest is about the same, good solid A minus student, good test scores, that's what they're looking for, and the parents paid a lot of money for those schools. I don't know what the numbers were for each, but yeah it wasn't just the super league schools.

Andy: Yeah that was interesting to me. So let me ask you the juicy stuff, so when you were at Princeton, did anyone ever solicit you or anyone that you knew to try get in the side door, the back door or anything other than the front door?

Don: No, never when I was at Princeton. I've had one case from a Chinese family ask that question, since I become an independent counselor, but no I never had anything like that while I was at Princeton.

Don: I did have some of my admissions colleagues ask occasionally, put it this way, what they would get for development list that would came down, and some of the time the admitted the kids and sometimes they didn't.

Don: I'm not going to mention names but one time we had an application from the son of very wealthy guy, and the guy's promise was going to be a reasonably sized gift. The kid wasn't that bad, he was form Texas, I remember specifically, because the admissions counselor showed me the kid's application, and he was okay, but he told me "Well, there's just something about this guy I don't like, I think he's a little spoiled, I think he's this I think he's that, I'm just not going to admit him." And that probably meant some millions of dollars down the line, but that was his decision, and he just didn't think he'd be a good fit for Princeton so he was denied.

Don: I'm sure there were many others going on like that, that I didn't know personally, but that's the thing admissions people are still the ones that are making these decisions no matter what the SAT, no matter what the money might be, what the athletic prowess is, whatever.

Don: But it looks like this guy (Singer) made it so he would make sure at the admissions level there was enough there on a positive side and no negative flags, that he was pretty sure these kids were getting in. I don't know whether all these kids actually got into the schools that all the publicity's about I haven't seen much about that, I thought I saw somewhere that the Stanford sailing case that Stanford didn't have a record of the student, I don't know you may know more about that.

Andy: Yeah so the story was that he was admitted but deferred for a year, and then he decided not to go at all. So then the sailing coach contacted Singer, and said " I've another spot that just opened up" for another kid.

Don: Oh okay alright. So he was admitted there then. And the Yale soccer player, do we know that girl was admitted? I don't know.

Andy: I don't remember.

Andy: So back to the scenario you just described about the Chinese businessman, next, the brother contacted you, what happened next?

Don: Yeah the father was in China, and I don't think he spoke English, so the brother was in the US and told me that the father wants to know, what it would take to get her admitted. I said there's really no way to tie any gift to

29

any admissions decisions, but if he has a cause and a school he wants to give money to and he wants it for the department of Chinese History or whatever, he can go ahead and do that, his daughter can apply there, but I can't say that she'll necessarily be admitted there. That was the way that conversation went. We talked for a while, he hung up and that's the last I heard of it.

Andy: Was he surprised, because when I have similar conversations and tell any affluent client, whether from the US, or another country, substantially the same thing, they seem not to really believe me.

Don: Yeah I think he might have been surprised, yeah. Him being here in America, he probably was not as surprised as the father was. The father probably felt he could do that. But yeah, he kept asking the question again and again in different ways, so I think to some extent he was surprised.

Andy: In the recent past I've seen stories about consultants who took seven figure fees and guaranteed their clients admission into Harvard, and then it didn't happen and they were sued. *[See Chinese Parents Sue Consultant After Sons Are Rejected by Harvard, New York Times, October 11 2012]*

Don: Yeah that came out a couple years ago, was it a couple million dollars, something like that.

Andy: Yeah. That was when I first raised my rates, I don't know about you.

Don: No not at all.

Andy: Moving right along, I think another thing that is almost as rampant and wide spread as the un-timed testing accommodations, and other accommodations has to do with my favorite quotes that I ever heard you say about the college application: "There's a difference between 'polish' and 'fiction'." I'm talking about the college activity section or the resume. I keep hearing about a lot of kids, and I've been approached also, who just make up stuff, they'll say "oh my dad's friend said that I could put down that I work for him over the summer should I do that?" And my response is always "First of all it's not going to get you into college or not, so why even have this discussion; Second of all that's lying, you don't need to do that." But it's just *the assumption behind the question that is so troubling* - that everyone is doing it, so should I just do this and this is what it takes. So have you encountered that?

Don: In a way I have, I look at all the stuff, I always go over the kids Common App before it goes in, and I've talked to them for a year or so, so I know it's pretty much legitimate, so I guess I don't get any sense of let me jazz this up a little bit, I guess they've been pretty straight.

Don: What I get from my foreign clients is a little bit different, is they're a little astonished that we have, fundamentally, an honor system. Because when I'm in China, they normally come in with a student and they bring a copy of every certificate and award and whatever, and they think all those things going to have to be made copies of and sent in with the admissions application.When I say, "No, you just write down what you've done and that's going to be it," they're really surprised. But I certainly hear about a lot of maneuvering going on by American students, I hear plenty of stories about it.

Don: In China, there's the SAT gambit, where there's pretty wide spread cheating on the SAT, and then I'm sure it goes   into   other   people   writing   teachers recommendations, some of the teachers don't speak very good English, so the agency over there writes the

31

recommendations, I've even heard some transcripts, the transcripts aren't quite as readily available as they are over here, so they make up. So I think because it is an honor system, it's much easier than what those guys, Singer did, it's really relatively easy to make up basically this fake application, by way of writing the essays, doing the teachers recs, coming up with a transcript, and basically find a way to get those SAT scores up high, an early copy of the exam which sometimes shows up. Or I've had students who...do you want me to keep going on, I've never talked so much.

Andy: Yeah yeah.

Don: In China, the SAT is given in Hong Kong, and some of these agencies over there, (what they call college consultants, big business agencies), they send students to Australia to take the SAT which I think is about four or five hours earlier than Hong Kong, then they send in the answers to the kids before the go in the Hong Kong test. So this is a pretty elaborate cheating schemes. They simply got an early copy. Also, for a while, the College Board was actually repeating earlier (domestic) tests later on the international market, so these companies would find out that it was the same test and they would start then teaching in their test prep course as to the exact test they were going to be taking.

Don: Anyway, the whole point is, because if the honor system, it's really easy to take advantage of, and for International students, in China where they don't have all the same things and you wouldn't have to do anything nearly as elaborate as this guy Singer did in the US.

Andy: Yeah that story was also in the news less than a year ago taking earlier tests and getting the answers and funneling it into China and to America I think.

Don: And yet we get back to the parents role in this, and why they would do this, and how much money they spend, and why is it so important to them for these students to go to certain colleges It's really fascinating, you and I rely on it probably in our business because they want to do more than just go through the high school counselors.

Don: And it's particularly important in China, India, Korea, Japan or whatever, the *US News & World Report* is their bible, as you probably know, I know you've dealt with some Chinese and Indian students, they just go down that list school by school and they think there's a big difference between number 3 and number 13 and number 33. And it's very very important to them as to where the schools are on that list, because they have that outcome in mind. Then it's what they have to do to get there, to have a chance.

Don: For some families, we're still talking about a relatively small number of kids and parents who do this, but since there's so many applications over there (internationally), the admissions people in the US are very careful about looking at some of these applications. Most of the times they setting up interviews and Skype calls to see whether that applicant is the same person represented on the application, and they're doing some very elaborate checking. But I think overall the numbers are much larger and the problem much deeper in the international market.

Andy: Interesting, okay.

Andy: So to loop back to the resume and the activity sheet, if a kid makes up some sort of job, award, being captain of a team, being a founder of a robotics team, or something like that, and puts that on Common Application, that the guidance counselor is also signing off on, what are the implications, and how likely are they to get caught?

Don: The counselor just sends in a transcript and usually the school report and a few other things, the counselor in most cases will not actually see the Common App. There's no in-school systematic review of what the kid puts on a Common App. So truly, it's the honor system, they way they (admissions officers) have to watch out is for inconsistencies. Let's say they're on the robotics team and they say they're the founder, the president and they won a national competition. And then they end up asking their physics teacher to write a recommendation, and the recommendation say he's a contributing member of the robotics team but doesn't do much or whatever. Or same way with English, he's taken honors English and getting a B, but writes the world's greatest essay, or something like that so I think that there are some internal checks when a student is making some "short cuts." we'll call them. But I think for the most part the chance are they'll probably get away with most of this, put it that way.

Andy: Okay that's depressing, thanks.

Andy: So what about guidance counselor recommendations, how many of them are, I don't want to say "negative," but they're not all glowing and positive, is that fair to say? How are they used by every school as an indicator of a kid's ability and character. Do some schools use them more than others, what's your take?

Don: Yeah so there's the school report, so the transcript goes in and, with that is a school report and they write some comments. So the guidance counselor usually writes a paragraph or two. A lot of those come from what's called "Brag Sheets," the school sends a sheet to the parent, a sheet to a kid, and they actually write what they do, and so the guidance counselor in many cases takes what the student says and put that in the school report, the counselor recommendation. The there's usually two teachers that write, now that's Independent of that, and now it's what the kid does in that class, now for the students I'm dealing with, you wouldn't ask a teacher to write for you if they don't like, done a really poor job or whatever.

Andy: You would think.

Don: There's a lot of grade inflation, and it's similar in recommendations, terms like "very good" almost becomes the average. And then it's these key words, there's exceptional, outstanding, one of the best or whatever, so there's a lot of expression there, and it really only makes a difference if you see something that's unusual. And the description that I have seen that probably makes a difference, would be "one of the few I've seen in my career." If you see that one in a rec, now he (the admissions officer) knows the kid is special. "One of the best I've seen in the last two or three years" is pretty strong and then after that they all read pretty much the same way. So you're looking for that extra comparison to really pay much attention otherwise you just zip through it and move on to other things.

Andy: So it's unusual to see something negative in a recommendation.

Don: Yeah once again I don't choose the recommendations, but what I would think, it's very rare to see something negative, unless the kid makes a mistake and a teacher is kind of out to get him for some reason. I would say it's very very rare that a recommendation, it might be a very mild negative, he could work harder, he doesn't quite apply himself, but to really torpedo the kid let's say that, I think that's really rare.

Andy: And do the smaller private liberal art schools take these recommendations into account more than the larger public and land grant universities?

Don: Definitely yeah, everything at the smaller college level is done more carefully than at the higher levels, yeah. That's when they really look at these things, they might even do the old-fashioned thing, of calling the guidance counselor and finding more about things. Which almost never takes place now at the larger universities. The old-fashioned way of doing admissions is now pretty much reserved for the high quality small colleges, who are getting maybe 5000 applications, while these other schools are getting 30, 40, 50 thousand applications, and they're just getting through them in a hurry, there's no question about it.

Don: And if you talk about the big public's, what does UCLA have, 100,000 applications, they're doing a lot of computer screening for probably at least half of those (applications). Unless they're flagged for some special characteristic, there not even going to look at their activities or their essays of things like that. And then when they get down to this other levels, a more manageable group, that's when I think they start digging into more holistic admissions.

Don: That's the impression get for the large systems.

Andy: That is accurate as far as I know. We have four former college admissions officers that work with us and help our kids and they've told me that repeatedly.

Andy: What do you think happens next, in terms of schools changing policies, College Board changing policies, regulation, anything.

Don: I don't know quite, so let's look at two things, there's test cheating and there's accommodations and test cheating goes together, there's the athletic submission.

Don: So the athletes are still going to get priority, maybe there's someone else that looks at these things a little carefully, maybe there's now going to be a little double-checking, so someone like the associate AD at USC doesn't have sole responsibility. Maybe a little internal stuff on the athletic part of things, to make sure that's carefully done.

Don: And the testing side I think is a very unique and sometimes clever way of getting around all the other checks they have. So I don't see anything long lasting there, in a way what the College Board does.

Don: As far as the accommodations go, I think for a while there's going to be some talk about cracking down some way on that, but I don't see any deep long lasting changes coming out of this, I really don't.

Andy: How about donations made for a kid who's applying to that particular college, do you think that'll continue?

Don: Yeah I think so. I see there was some group that's called for, actually the center of a representative calling for some taking away tax deductions if the kid is admitted at the same time. I don't know how you could possibly enforce anything like that, but then you'll have business organizations and foundations probably won't go for that, so I think that one will die down. I don't know how you could possibly control that through the taxes or anywhere else. So yeah once again I could be wrong but once again I don't see any deep long lasting effect, but I do see a careful look at all the different aspects of this, and colleges in their own way, or the College Board will see if they can do maybe in some way to cut this out, but the guy (Singer) really did find some way to get around, if you cheat you're going to cheat, how hard they try to cover, people who want to do that at that high level of sophistication and change things in a way that basically would make it harder for just your regular kids right.

Andy: Yeah.

Don: That you don't want to do, you don't want to put anything so restrictive to catch people like this, that's going to make it hard for the very kids that you want to keep the door open for.

Andy: Right it's the whole baby out with the bathwater thing. You don't want to unduly have a chilling effect on the kids that really deserve to get in.

Andy: Alright final question, what it's your advice for "regular" families that we're talking about, or any family that's applying to school, going forward on any of this stuff, does anything change, is it still the same advice, can you think of anything that you would say differently now?

Don: No, no I really don't think so. As you know, we do the best we can with these students I think, honesty is the best policy, you may not get in that super dream school but you'll probably go to a school that you'll do very well in, you'll fit in well, and I tell these kids that are so intent on going to the top whatever, top 20 top 30 it's still how you perform at the school you go to. And if you're going to go on in life and you're going to go on in your job, you're much better coming out with your A average and doing really well, let's say if you're at New Jersey, at Rutgers and getting your job and doing well, rather than let's say going to a more prestigious school, just muddling through, getting a B, and then I don't think you'll probably do as well down the line. The over emphasis on prestige is everything, and my life will be better if I go to this school verse that school, I just spent an awful lot of time trying to talk parents out of that and I'll continue to do so.

Andy: Yeah, my version of that conversation is, that there's really no correlation between where you go and how successful you're going to be, no matter how you imagine including monetarily, I'm sure you've seen that study by Krueger and Dale, that tracks kids from elite and non-elite colleges and their success after college.

Don: Yeah exactly it's what you do when you get there and then what you do with it when you get out, yeah I'm a firm believer in that.

Andy: And in any given year there's a very large percentage of Harvard, Yale, Princeton etcetera graduates who are unemployed for various reasons. It's not guaranteed that just cause you go to one of these schools...

Don: Exactly yeah.

Andy: Well that was great, I really appreciate all the time you spent and your advice and your take on this!

For more information on how to use Mr. Betterton's "College Guru" software, which predicts odds of admission for each college on your list with approximately 90% accuracy, go to www.LockwoodInnerCircle.com

CHAPTER 4

IS BERNIE BEHIND THE NEW SAT "ADVERSITY SCORE" CHANGES?

The College Board, the "nonprofit" (hah!) behind the SAT, announced that it was reintroducing an "adversity score" to its scoring system.

In short, kids who come from disadvantaged neighborhoods will receive some sort of behind-the-scenes, double-secret notation on their SAT file for colleges to use as they see fit.

Although this policy appears to fall short of adding "bonus points" for social engineering purposes, or something that Bernie or AOC would propose, it sure feels like it.

Don't get me wrong, I believe that we need to do more to make education accessible to low-income and disadvantaged families. I just don't think the College Board did anything here.

Here's what I believe to be the real, hidden reason behind the announcement: to make us FEEL more kindly disposed to the good ol' College Board. I don't see it doing much else.

Why?

First, college admissions officers already do what the College Board is attempting to pull off with this policy. Admissions committees go out of their way to recruit kids from low income and disadvantaged families.

(Sure, they also favor legacies, student-athletes and photoshopped student-athletes, but work with me here).

Is it "fair" for admissions personnel to favor certain special categories, instead of sticking solely to academic merits?

There's no easy answer. As you may already know, it's being litigated currently by way of a lawsuit by an Asian American student with perfect scores who was denied admission to Harvard.

This meritocracy/social engineering controversy is also being played out in elite New York City high schools such as Stuyvesant and Bronx Science, which require children to perform extremely well on standardized tests to be admitted. Very few African-American kids scored well enough to get in. That could indicate problems with the testing process, or with the education they're getting in elementary or middle school.

My take on whether this should be permissible:

It's the wrong thing to focus on. We'd all be better off concentrating our energies on the stuff we can control.

Speaking as a parent, I would not want one of my children to feel insecure from wondering if they only way they got into a certain college or notched a certain achievement was because of some "unfair" advantage bestowed on them. In a way, I feel sorry for the kids caught up in the college scandal, who can't be feeling too great about themselves.

None of this is "fair." But life isn't fair either.

But forget about my take. The College Board can do whatever it wants, but I don't think anyone reviewing admissions statistics a year from now, or five years from now, will notice any discernible change in academic profiles of admitted students. I predict business as usual.

Actually, this announcement strikes me as a thinly-disguised effort for the College Board to address legitimate criticism that high income students who pay for test prep have an advantage over less fortunate peers.

Is that unfair? Of course it is. But the College Board hasn't claimed in years that the SAT was the great leveler, a pure "aptitude test," that couldn't be gamed. (The "A" in SAT used to stand for Aptitude, until the College Board dropped it.)

They used to argue that you couldn't increase your aptitude scores by studying, but not any more. Too many test prep operations like ours proved them wrong, time and again.

The announcement was also suspiciously close in time to the very public egg on the face of the College Board, thanks to the Felicity-Lori college scandal, which highlighted the apparent ease college consultant Rick Singer was able to get his clients accommodations to take their SATs untimed or with extra time, infiltrate certain College Board-sanctioned testing centers and bribe proctors.

Yowza. I'd want to change the conversation too.

Not to mention growing criticism in general that the SAT - and ACT - should go away entirely. (No way, if you want my prediction. Too much money involved.)

In summary, I see this announcement as the same type of tactic that any savvy politician would use to divert attention away from negative coverage - the College Board is attempting to change the news cycle with this public relations gambit.

What does this mean, going forward, for Forgotten Middle Class test-takers, who don't qualify for Favored Nation status under the new College Board guidelines? Will they have to achieve even higher scores, since they're arguably being penalized for NOT being in a special category?

I hope not. But it's unclear for now, only time will tell.

CHAPTER 5

STUPID ADVICE

Well-intentioned parents, guidance counselors and others will at some point, if they haven't already, tell you, Don't worry! Don't stress out!

I always thought this was stupid.

Seriously, who would be stressed if they could help it?

"Don't stress out, Samantha."

"Oh, Ok, thanks. I hadn't thought about that."

Why shouldn't you be a little anxious? Your future is unclear. You're encountering uncertainty about a major decision in uncharted waters.

Unless you've been living in a cave, you're slammed in the pie-hole daily with emails, direct mail and other relentless marketing from numerous ahem, "non-profit institutions of higher education."

Maybe you visited a college recently, and sat in on a prospective student "information session" (i.e. Sales Pitch).

Remember that 1/8th Comanche, Intel Finalist with the Olympic silver medal in Rowing, 2380 SATs, 17 APs (his school offered 18 but he had a conflict with the syndicated talk show he created and hosts) who was born without a kidney and is legally blind?

Wait-listed at BU.

The scene at your local high school isn't exactly "relaxing." Chances are you're confronted with things like:

- Overburdened, sleep-deprived kids loading up on AP exams and extra-curriculars designed to "package" themselves favorably for top colleges

- Kids spending their precious moments of downtime on $250 per hour SAT tutors (whose names are often shrouded in secrecy by parents lest other, competitor-kids get the same "edge")

- Hyper parents trolling message boards like College Confidential in the wee small hours of the morning, then sharing their discoveries (A valedictorian from Chappaqua with a 1580 got waitlisted at Northeastern! Can you believe it?) at the gym, soccer field or bar mitzvah

- Non-top tier colleges like Drexel eclipsing the $65,000 per year barrier

But you can manage your stress. "Compartmentalize" it, meaning, put it in its place, where it belongs.

Bruce Lee, the martial artist[4], talked about visualizing his problems on a piece of paper. He'd then picture himself crumpling it up and tossing it away.

Sound simplistic? It does to me too. But try it.

Getting your shinola together will also help. Meaning that if you feel overwhelmed, or have so much loaded on your plate that you don't know where to start, you will start feeling better instantly when you take action.

Here's what I mean. Make a list of all the stuff you've got to get done. (I recommend an old fashioned legal pad and pen, but if you prefer thumb typing your notes, so be it.)

---

[4] Yes, THAT Bruce Lee (I felt that I had to provide context).

Then, go through your list and identify the three most important items.

Then DO 'em! Don't stop until you're done.

(That last directive, "do" it, is admittedly simple, but critically important. Nothing happens until you MOVE. So no more analysis paralysis, over thinking or complaining. Your shit won't get done by itself.)

How do you determine your top priorities when they all seem pressing?

The ONLY way to decide is to think about what your goal is. Then you need to be ruthless and a cold-hearted son of a bitch[5] when it comes to focusing on the essential, and stripping away the crud that gets in your way.

Example: Let's say you want to get top grades so you can get into a great college. You (the new introspective you) have figured out the amount of studying you need to do in order to master the class material you've been taught.

So Priority 1 is getting your tush in a seat behind your desk and hitting the books! Don't stop until you're through.

And all of those distractions that creep in?

DEAD to me! (Actually, you.)

Shut off your stupid smart phone. Close down your Instagram and Finsta, Snappychat and XBox.

What about if you have conflicts, like lacrosse practice versus another extracurricular activity?

There's no easy answer. You have to come up with your own value system and make decisions accordingly.

---

[5] Or, "daughter of a bitch" if appropriate

Are you an athletic stud who is potentially going to play in college? Or are you a casual jock with no chance of playing post-high school.

If you fall into the latter category, it may not be that big a deal to skip the occasional practice in light of a conflict.

Blame me if your coach or teammates rip you a new one!

The point is that you will have to make choices, which for sure is difficult, but having a overriding purpose or set of goals will help you decide.

Here's another stress-busting technique for grades, tests, projects, etc., ask yourself What's the worst that can happen?

Let's say you get a C on a test, or don't get into Yale. So what?

Are you sentenced to a life of loser-dom if you weren't admitted to your top choice college? Far from it.

Modern history is loaded with examples of successful, famous people rejected from their top choice schools: legendary investor Warren Buffett, longtime news anchor Tom Brokaw, Nobel Laureates and numerous accomplished, productive folks.

History is also littered with successful people who never even went to college: Rockefeller, Carnegie, Sir Richard Branson, Zuckerberg, Jobs and Gates (OK, those last three dropped out of college).

Sometimes Plan B is much better than Plan A! Look at PayPal, which used to make software for an ancient device called the Palm Pilot, before they pivoted and go into the pay by email business.

Samsung was in a farming-related industry before it started making electronic products.

What if you got into a bunch of colleges, but can't decide where to go?

What's the worst that can happen? You pick a school, then realize you're unhappy?

Transfer! You may not think it's ideal, but you wouldn't be the first kid to do it.

Call me crazy, but I reject the idea that there's a perfect college for each kid.

Instead, I believe that there are six "perfect" colleges for every applicant. Maybe dozens.

So it seems kind of silly to me when kids obsess over getting into their "top choice" college.

Final point: go ahead and feel stressed, but make sure you put stress in its place. Your worst case scenario really isn't that bad.

CHAPTER 6

WHY GO?

I'm going to go out on a limb and wager that you're reading this book because you believe that a college degree will help you or your child succeed in life.

It's not the best business model for a college counselor to suggest "College ain't for everybody," but I feel it's worth discussing the value of a degree.

This ground has been trampled over by many smarter and better than I, so I want to suggest a few other ways of looking at the value of a college degree, on Planet Earth, TODAY.

As I write this in 2019, and when I wrote the original version of this book, *The Incomparable Applicant* in mid 2014, jobs are on most people's minds.

Just this morning, over a typical relaxing, quiet breakfast at home with my four docile, well-mannered children, I half-read another one of those articles about how it's better to have a college degree than not, because those with a degree are far less likely to be unemployed than those without a sheepskin! (There are many statistics proving this -although the earnings gap between degreed and non-degreed people is narrowing - but I'll spare you the full discussion.)

The kicker was buried midway down the piece: many college grads were working in jobs that don't require college degrees. One study claimed that 50% of college grads were employed in non-degree fields two years after graduating!

On the other hand, there's a shortage of electricians, plumbers and other similar service providers.

The Center for College Affordability reported that 115,000 custodians had college bachelor's degrees.

Nothing against custodians, they are among the most underappreciated employees anywhere. I spent several hours per week in college doing janitor work-study jobs, it was not exactly glamorous or attractive to other students.

One of the coolest aspects of our college consulting business is that about 50% of our clients are self-employed in a huge variety of businesses. We see everyone's tax returns and other financial information.

Our clients include doctors, lawyers and accountants. And plumbers, electricians and auto body shop owners.

Frequently, the second group is doing better, financially!

You'd be surprised at who's really wealthy, and who doesn't have two nickels to rub together. I'll leave it at that, but if you want more information on why, read *The Millionaire Next Door by Thomas Stanley*.

Back to the article: in summary, the good news is that it's easier to find work with a college degree. The bad news is that you don't need one for a lot of the jobs that are available.

If you have a boatload of student loans to pay off while you're waiting tables or serving half-caff soy mochachinos, you may not be better off than someone who never went to college who's working the shift before you.

But I'm not one of these guys who thinks that the purpose of going to college is to get a job, like a trade school. Although it would absolutely blow to get out of school with $150,000-plus of loans and not have any prospects.

I question whether it's worth paying more for some colleges than others, in the hopes that prestige or other factors will make chances of post-college success greater.

I'm asked this question frequently, in the form of Is it worth the extra $30,000 per year to attend Duke instead of SUNY Binghamton (or other state's flagship public university)?

There are at least two ways to look at this question. On one hand, an oft-cited study[6] shows that kids who were admitted to both a prestigious college and a state university, but chose the state university, are just as financially successful as their counterparts who went the prestige college route.

On the other hand, there's an argument that I think about in terms of my wife's experience.

Pearl attended Skidmore College (she transferred to Cornell after her freshman year).

The guy down the hall from her came from a successful family – his dad was Ralph Lauren. Pearl's friend went to SUNY Binghamton, the "public Ivy" of New York State. The girl on her hall's father was an accountant in Bellmore.

Personally, I don't attribute too much weight to the "you'll meet a higher quality of person" at a private school thought, but I can't deny that it's true. You're bound to find more upper crust students from affluent families at upper crust, private colleges.

I just don't know that it's worth an extra 30 G's per year to attend a snooty private college when you could attend your local state school instead.

---

[6] Google 'Dale and Krueger"

CHAPTER 7

CONVERSATION WITH A BILLIONAIRE

Earlier this year, I ran into the only billionaire that I know, sadly.

Saul is the father of one of Pearl's friends from high school. (He was attending his grandson's play (once, instead of four times like I had to, I mean, "got to"), which my kids were in also.

We chit-chatted before "curtain" and then he turned to the topic of my cute, paltry business (at least that's how I felt, Saul's too nice to be condescending).

I just don't understand how parents justify spending $250,000 on their kids' college education. It's crazy - it's not worth it!

Of course I agreed, although that amount is probably a rounding error for him.

I asked Saul where he went to college.

He graduated from City College, when tuition was zero. And he endured a big controversy when they raised it to $50!

Saul later earned postgraduate degrees from other institutions, including NYU and M.I.T., before founding several technology companies and becoming a full-time investor.

He mentioned a recent meeting with two other prominent businessmen, one a famous software entrepreneur and owner of a local professional sports team, the other a similarly successful businessman.

We figured out that we had all been at City College at the same time! he chuckled.

I said that didn't surprise me, because, on any given list of Fortune 100 CEO's, about 33% attended elite, "pedigreed" colleges and the balance went to other schools, or didn't go at all. Times Higher Education, a British publication researched the educational backgrounds of the CEO's of the top 500 companies in the world.

Yes, there were plenty of top schools represented (Harvard, Columbia, Stanford,) but so were schools like University of Texas-Austin, Texas A&M, Michigan State, Georgia Tech and Auburn.[7]

Look at some of the 173 undergraduate colleges represented by Harvard Law School's 1L's (first year students)[8]:

American University

American University in Bulgaria

Arizona State University

Ateneo de Manila University

---

[7] You can do your own search ("Alma Maters of Fortune 500 CEOs and find a bunch of articles like this, which all pretty much draw the same conclusion: https://www.usnews.com/education/best-colleges/articles/2018-06-11/top-fortune-500-ceos-where-they-went-to-college)

[8]   From   https://hls.harvard.edu/dept/jdadmissions/apply-to-harvard-law-school/undergraduate-colleges/

Auburn University

Babeş-Bolyai University

Babson College

Bard College

Bates College

Baylor University

Beth Medrash Govoha

Biola University

Boston College

Bowdoin College

Brandeis University

Brigham Young University

Brown University

Bryn Mawr College

California State Polytechnic University – Pomona

Carnegie Mellon University

Case Western Reserve University

China Foreign Affairs University

Colgate University

College of the Holy Cross

College of William And Mary

Columbia University

Cornell University

Creighton University

Dartmouth College

Davidson College

Drexel University

Duke University

Duquesne University

Emory University

Ewha Womans University

Fairleigh Dickinson University

Fordham University

Franklin Marshall College

Furman University

George Washington University

Georgetown University

Grinnell College

Harvard College

Haskell Indian Nations University

Haverford College

Hobart and William Smith Colleges

Hofstra University

Howard Payne University

Howard University

Illinois State University

Indiana University Bloomington

Johns Hopkins University

Kansas State University

King's College London

Koç University

Marquette University

Maryland Institute College of Art

Massachusetts Institute Technology

McGill University

McMaster University

Miami University

Middlebury College

Moravian College

Morehouse College

New Jersey Institute of Technology

New York University

New York University – Abu Dhabi

Northeastern University

Northern Arizona University

Northwest Missouri State University

Northwestern University

Oberlin College

Oklahoma Christian University

Peking University

Pennsylvania State University

Pepperdine University

Pomona College

Princeton University

Queens College – CUNY

Queen's University

Reed College

Rensselaer Polytechnic Institute

Rice University

Rutgers State University – Newark

Sciences Po

Shanghai Jiao Tong University

Skidmore College

Smith College

St. Mary's College of Maryland

Stanford University

SUNY Binghamton

SUNY College of Environmental Science and Forestry

Swarthmore College

Syracuse University

Texas A&M University

Texas Christian University

The King's College (NYC)

The Ohio State University

Touro College

Tsinghua University

Tufts University

Tulane University

United States Coast Guard Academy

United States Military Academy

Universidade de Sao Paulo

University of Miami

University of Alabama

University of Arizona

University of British Columbia

University of California – Berkeley

University of California – Davis

University of California – Los Angeles

University of California – San Diego

University of California – Santa Barbara

University of California – Santa Cruz

University of Cambridge

University of Chicago

University of Connecticut

University of Delaware

University of Edinburgh

University of Florida

University of Georgia

University of Hawai'i – Mānoa

University of Hawaii – West Oahu

University of Illinois

University of Kansas

University of Kentucky

University of Leeds

University of Maryland

University of Michigan – Ann Arbor

University of Michigan – Dearborn

University of Minnesota

University of Montana

University of Nebraska

University of Nevada – Las Vegas

University of North Carolina – Chapel Hill

University of North Carolina – Charlotte

University of Notre Dame

University of Oklahoma

University of Ottawa

University of Oxford

University of Pennsylvania

University of Pittsburgh

University of Saskatchewan

University of Science and Technology of China

University of Southern California

University of Tennessee – Chattanooga

University of Tennessee – Knoxville

University of Texas – Dallas

University of Texas – Austin

University of Texas – San Antonio

University of Toronto

University of Tulsa

University of Utah

University of Victoria

University of Virginia

University of Washington

University of Waterloo

University of Zimbabwe

Vanderbilt University

Vassar College

Virginia Commonwealth University

Virginia Tech

Washington University in St. Louis

Waynesburg University

Wellesley College

Wesleyan University

Wheaton College

Wichita State University

Williams College

Yale University

Yeshiva University

York University

Side note - I haven't heard of many of these schools. Babeș-Bolyai University? It's in Romania, that must be why.

If you searched the undergraduate institutions that sent kids to Harvard Business School[9], you'd see the same sort of mix of top, prestigious undergraduate schools and other, "regular" schools such as:

American University of Beirut

American University of Cairo

Amherst College

Anna University

Arizona State University

Ateneo De Manila University

Babson College

Barnard College

Bates College

Ben Gurion University

Bentley College

Bilkent University

Birla Institute of Technology and Science

Bob Jones University

Bocconi University

Bogazici University

Boston College

Boston University

Bowdoin College

Brandeis University

---

[9]   https://www.hbs.edu/mba/admissions/class-profile/Pages/undergraduate-institutions.aspx

Brigham Young University

Brooklyn Polytechnic Institute

Brown University

Bryn Mawr College

California Institute of Technology

Carleton College

Carnegie Mellon University

Case Western Reserve University

Catholic University of Louvain

Chinese University of Hong Kong

Chulalongkorn University

College of Management - Academic Studies

College of the Holy Cross

Colorado School of Mines

Columbia University

Cornell University

Dartmouth College

Dickinson College

Duke University

Ecole Centrale

Ecole Nationale Superieure de Chimie de Paris - ParisTech

Ecole Polytechnique

Ecole Spéciale des Travaux Publics

Ecole Superieure Science Economic Commerce (Initial Period)

Emory University

EPITA Graduate School of Computer Science

ESCP Paris

Etseib

Florida A&M University

Florida State University

Franklin W. Olin College

Fudan University

Fundacao Getulio Vargas - Sao Paulo Business School

Georgetown University

Georgia Institute of Technology

Georgia Southern University

GIK Institute of Engineering Sciences and Technology

Gujarat University

H.R. College of Commerce and Economics

Hampton University

Harvard University

Harvey Mudd College

Haverford College

Hebrew University of Jerusalem

Heidelberg College

Hochschule St. Gallen

Howard University

Humboldt University of Berlin

Imperial College of Science and Technology

Indian Institute of Technology, Bombay

Indian Institute of Technology, Kanpur

Indian Institute of Technology, Kharagpur

Indian Institute of Technology, Madras

Indian Institute of Technology, New Delhi

Indiana University

Insper Ibmec-SP

Institut Nationale des Sciences Appliquées Toulouse

Instituto Superior Tecnico

Instituto Tecnologico Autonomo de Mexico

Instituto Tecnologico de Aeronautica

Instituto Tecnologico de Buenos Aires

Instituto Tecnologico de Monterrey (ITESM)

Integrale Institut d'enseignement superieur prive

Interdisciplinary Center

IQS School of Engineering - Universitat Ramon Llull

Jadavpur University

Jiao Tong University

Johns Hopkins University

Keio University

Kettering University

Korea University

Lahore University of Management Sciences

London School of Economics and Political Science

Louisiana State University

Loyola University, Chicago

Lycée Privé Sainte Geneviève

Lycee Saint Louis

Maastricht University

Macalester College

Massachusetts Institute of Technology

McGill University

Michigan State University

Middlebury College

Milan Polytechnic

Monash University

Montana State University

Morehouse College

Moscow Institute of Physics and Technology

Moscow State Univ of Economics, Statistics, and Informatics

Moscow State University

Mount Holyoke College

National Institute of Technology, Karnataka

National Research University - Higher School of Economics

National Taiwan University

National Tsing Hua University

New York University

North Carolina State University

Northeastern University

Northwestern University

Norwegian School of Economics and Business Administration

Oberlin College

Ohio Northern University

Ohio State University

Ohio Wesleyan University

Oxford University

Peking University

Pennsylvania State University

Peoples Education Society Institute of Technology

Pontificia Universidad Catolica de Chile

Pontificia Universidade Catolica do Rio de Janeiro

Princeton University

Punjab Engineering College, Deemed University

Purdue University

Qinghua University

Queen's University

Randolph-Macon College

Rensselaer Polytechnic Institute

Rice University

Rijksuniversiteit Gent

Rutgers - The State University

Saint John's College

Santa Clara University

SASTRA University

Seattle University

Seoul National University

Shri Ram College of Commerce

Simon Fraser University

Southern Methodist University

St. Joseph University

Stanford University

State University - Higher School of Economics

State University of New York, Binghamton

Stockholm School of Economics

Swarthmore College

Swiss Federal Institute of Technology

Syracuse University

Technical University of Budapest

Technion-Israel Institute of Technology

Technische Universität München

Tel Aviv University

Tel-Aviv University

Texas A&M University

Thammasat University

The College of William and Mary

The George Washington University

The Interdisciplinary Center - IDC

Tufts University

Tulane University

Unicamp-Brazil

United States Air Force Academy

United States Military Academy

United States Naval Academy

Universidad de los Andes

Universidad Pompeu Fabra (UPF)

Universidad Pontificia de Comillas (ICADE)

Universidad Torcuato Di Tella

Universidade de Sao Paulo

Universidade Federal do Parana

Universidade Federal do RGS

University College London

University of Alberta

University of Arizona

University of Bombay

University of British Columbia

University of Buenos Aires

University of California, Berkeley

University of California, Los Angeles

University of Cambridge

University of Cape Town

University of Chicago

University of Chile

University of Cincinnati

University of Connecticut

University of Delaware

University of Delhi

University of Edinburgh

University of Florida

University of Georgia

University of Iceland

University of Illinois

University of Kansas

University of Maine

University of Mannheim

University of Maryland

University of Maryland, Baltimore County

University of Massachusetts

University of Melbourne

University of Miami

University of Michigan

University of Minnesota

University of Montreal

University of Münster

University of Nebraska

University of New South Wales

University of North Carolina

University of Notre Dame

University of Oklahoma

University of Oxford

University of Paris II

University of Pennsylvania

University of Pittsburgh

University of Poona

University of Queensland

University of Saint Thomas

University of San Andres

University of Sheffield

University of South Carolina

University of Southern California

University of St. Gallen

University of Sydney

University of Texas

University of the Basque Country - Faculty of Engineering

University of the Philippines

University of the South

University of Tokyo

University of Toronto

University of Utah

University of Virginia

University of Warwick

University of Washington

University of Waterloo

University of Western Australia

University of Western Ontario

University of Wisconsin

Vanderbilt University

Vassar College

Vienna School of Economics and Business Administration

Virginia Commonwealth University

Virginia Military Institute

Visveswaraiah Technological University

Warsaw School of Economics

Waseda University

Washington and Lee University

Washington University

Webb Institute

Wellesley College

Wesleyan University

WHU – Otto Beisheim School of Management

Williams College

Yale University

Yeditepe University

Yonsei University

Zhejiang University

Disclaimer: I'm a huge fan of Chulalongkorn University, I pick them every year in the NCAA Men's Basketball tournament.[10]

Back to my conversation: I asked Saul if things were different today, since he had sent his own son to an Ivy League college.

When we're hiring, we care about where they finish, not where they start, he said. I've heard similar comments from countless doctors and lawyers as well.

Saul felt that his son went to the wrong school and thought that schools like Baruch and Queens college (local, non-elite colleges in New York City) were great options for many families, still, and send many graduates to top jobs and graduate schools.

He nodded when I said it's easy to choose colleges based on what their peers suggest, and said that many kids - and parents - were foolish to overlook other options.

People like Saul, who rub elbows with some of the most successful people on the planet, understand that there's life outside of the "bubble."

---

[10] Kidding. It's in Thailand. Yes, I had to look that up.

And that going to a "brand" school doesn't guarantee ANYTHING.

The Wall Street Journal surveyed top recruiters to rank the best-qualified students by school and major. One IVY cracked the top 25: Cornell at number 14!

Here's the list:

Penn State

Texas A&M

University of Illinois Urbana-Champaign

Purdue

Arizona State

University of Michigan Ann-Arbor

Georgia Institute of Technology

University of Maryland

University of Florida

Carnegie Mellon

Brigham Young

Ohio State

Virginia Polytech

Cornell U

University of California-Berkeley

University of Wisconsin-Madison

UCLA

Texas Tech

NC State/University of Virginia (tie)

Rutgers

Notre Dame

MIT

USC

Washington State/UNC-Chapel Hill (tie)

What's the reason why employers (and recruiters) favor state schools? The Forbes article indicated that internships offered by state schools was the biggest factor.

If you haven't gotten the point yet, let's look at law school again, traditionally a sure-fire bet to gainful employment. Consider these law school unemployment statistics:

20.35% of Notre Dame law school graduates (ranked 23rd in the country by US News) are unemployed, according to The Atlantic. So is 10.3% of the University of Michigan Law School (#10), 11.6% of Duke Law School (#11), even 4.6% of Harvard Law (#2) grads.

Attending a prestigious college is no express train to success.

CHAPTER 8

CRINGEY STORY ABOUT HOW OUR KIDS PERFORM IN INTERVIEWS

Let me tell you a little story about a conversation that happened the day before I sat down to write this. Pearl and I were in the hospital, visiting my niece. She is just gave birth to her first child.

She is a successful corporate attorney, she's been working the same firm right out of law school, possibly four or five years, at this point. We somehow got to talking about some of the total losers that she interviewed for summer programs in her capacity as senior associate and assignment manager.

Sidebar: her own "College Story" is interesting. You know how Pearl and I always say "It doesn't matter where you start, it matters where you finish?" Here's a great example. When our niece was in high school, her top choice college was the University of Pennsylvania. She applied Early Decision, but didn't get in. She took it really hard, but I'm sparing you the details, including the basket of inappropriately adorned cookies we sent as a consolation.

Fast forward a few months later, she gets into the only other school she applied to, Michigan. Not too shabby of course, but not an Ivy where she saw herself belonging Maybe she had a little chip on her shoulder, so she graduates with honors, at the top of her class. She ends up getting into a top 10 law school.

From there, she ended up getting this great job at one of the biggest law firms in New York City, where she's thriving.

Incidentally, the head of the firm graduated SUNY Albany before going to law school at U Michigan and NYU Law. NOT Penn, Harvard or Stanford. Food for thought.

The question is, would she (and he) have gotten into that top law school had she instead attended an Ivy undergrad, where it would have been a lot harder for her to achieve high grades, because she would have been competing with kids who were probably a notch higher in academic caliber than the ones at Michigan?

You have to admit that it's debatable, don't get mad at me!

I call this "Playing the Long Game." Most kids - and people - are enmeshed in the short game, in our case, the four years. "Where are you applying?" "What's it ranked?" "Did you hear back?: "Where did you get in?"

But, the Long Game strategy could, just could, indicate that it's actually better NOT to go to such an uber-competitive undergraduate school, because you're more likely to have a higher GPA than if you want to an easier undergraduate program.

In the previous chapter I spun you a yarn about a family friend, the only billionaire I know (sadly), who told me something that's worth repeating here:

1. He went to City College (Tution: zero) before going to MIT for grad school

2. When he hires, he cares only about where the candidate finished - grad school - not where he started (undergrad)

3. He wishes that his own son went to a state school instead of Wharton, but that's where his kid wanted to go so he "let" him!

Another quickie: Our client, Gerry, an attorney. I'm working with his second daughter now. He was in my office several weeks ago, and told me about how when he graduated Georgetown, *magna cum laude*, he applied to Georgetown Law and didn't get in!

So he goes into the admissions office and says, "Guys, what the hell? How did you not admit me?"

They told him, "Well, we had to take kids from other undergraduate programs. We can't just take kids from our own undergraduate program."

Things worked out OK for Gerry, he's very successful. But you get the point, the Short Game isn't the important contest.

Okay. I'm done digressing. Back to the interview story.

My niece interviews budding summer associates who are applying after their first or second years of law school. These kids tend to be really, really high achieving, 3.8, 3.9 GPAs at super competitive law schools.

Which boggles the mind when you consider some of the exchanges that she has in these interviews. I'm going to share two of them, and throw in another one of my own for good measure.

Whether you're applying to law school, applying for a job, doing a college interview, interviewing for an internship, whatever, you have to be ready for some basic questions. Not only "Tell me about yourself," "Tell me about a favorite class," "Tell me about something you do outside for fun," but other, more open-ended ones.

One of the questions that you can't afford to blow is, "So, do you have any questions for us?" One guy told my niece, "Nope, I'm good. You've got a lot of information on the website. Thanks."

Here's a tip: you can't say that. That kind of question is a test to see whether you've spent time thinking about how and why that firm might be a good fit, whether you've researched your job opportunity, how you think, and, to a lesser extent, your social skills.

So "Nope!" won't cut it.

She asked that question to another candidate, also high-achieving. His answer: "Yeah, do you mind if I look at my notes here?"

"Of course," my niece responds.

So he proceeds to fumble around, and take out a yellow legal pad. He flips through a bunch of pages, resulting in an awkward pause of a half a minute or so. Finally, his eyes light up as he appears to find something, he looks up and says, "Oh, yeah! Tell me how you like working here."

THAT's the question you couldn't remember? That's the one you had to write down? Are you kidding me? Cringing.

The best story wasn't interview-related. It was about one particular summer associate who had to be told, "We don't order alcoholic drinks at lunch." The back story is that the summer associates go out twice a week at her firm with partners and associates. She didn't seem to pick up on the fact that no one else ordered alcohol. (The days of the three martini *Mad Men* era type lunch behavior are long gone, sadly. Sorry, Roger Sterling. :)

So after the second or third lunch where she ordered wine, someone said, "Hey, we don't do that at lunch here..

Her response, "That's okay, I do!"

Wow. One one hand, I respect the, ahem, "spine" on her. She could be the kind of attorney I'd want to hire, personally.

On the other hand, she alienated everyone at the firm that had a say in whether she'd get a job offer or not. She decided not to play the game, which of course is her prerogative.

My interview story: A client who owns a small advertising agency on the north shore of Long Island. We had a meeting, but he was late. He shows up, and apologizes, "Hey, I'm sorry I'm late. I was interviewing someone for work." Okay.

Then I noticed that he's sitting there with a half grin on his face, waiting for me to say something. "Well, aren't you going to ask me how the interview went?" he asks?

"Okay, Paul, how was the interview?" I asked.

Paul replied, "You mean with the candidate, or with her mother?"

"Are you you-know-whatting me?" I shouted (use your imagination).

Sadly, he wasn't. Even more sadly, that wasn't the first instance where he interviewed a candidate and the mom.

Okay. Back to the question. What does this all mean? A a couple of things.

One is really depressing. More anecdotal examples of the decline of American civilization. More dangerous than global warming or a 70% tax rate.

On the other hand, for my niece, my kids and your kids, this is actually a very good thing because it just shows how low the bar is set! It's great news! If you have half a brain and a modicum of social graces, you're going to stand out when you interview.

If you're able to make eye contact, shake hands with a relatively dry handshake, not stare at your phone, not answer your phone during an interview, not pick at various orifices on your face, et cetera (all real examples) you have an advantage over 95% of the morons you're competing with. If you're relatively calm, and perspiration-free, you take deep breaths, and you actually act like you're listening, and you ask questions, even better.

When your interviewer asks, "Do YOU have any questions for us?" you don't say, "Um, oh, I don't have any questions," or even worse, "Uh.." It's okay to have written notes, but it's not okay to be UNprepared.

Same idea for the college essays, which are analogous. When you're asked the question, "What is it about Boston University that inspired you to apply?" Or, "What is it about Delaware that made you want to apply?" You need to give *specific* examples. The more specific, the better. Be *convincing.*

My niece asked a candidate if he had questions, he came up with zilch. Couldn't he have taken a LITTLE time away from Fortnite or whatever he was doing to spend all of 30 minutes, at most, on the firm's website to find out about the practice areas, find out some of the big clients, find out the backgrounds of some of the other people who work there, and other key programs that they were involved with?

Likewise, you'll be under less pressure when you're writing essays, so it's even easier to go on their websites, spend 20 or 30 minutes scouring around trying to come up with things that are interesting to you, and somewhat unique, or actually unique about each college.

Then, you can give an answer along the lines of, "When I saw that Professor Such and Such, who has a background including serving as a communications director for three Fortune 500 companies, and I saw some of the courses that he teaches such as "Crisis Management Communications for Corporations..." that is a much more specific, "deeper" answer than, "I love Boston, your college is really highly ranked, there's a lot of internship opportunities in Boston, and your college is very reputable." The latter is a very high level, generic enough to apply to 40 schools and, most important, not going to help you get in. You need to go deep and demonstrate that you did your due diligence.

Whether on the college essay, college interview or any type of interview, it takes only a little effort to come off as convincing. Your job is to demonstrate that you're thoughtful, that you've done your homework, and you're able to match up what that particular college, or that potential employer, or internship provider has to offer you and vice versa. And how you can specifically help them, I might add.

CHAPTER 9

WHY GUIDANCE COUNSELORS HATE ME

It's not terribly uncommon for me to get hate mail from guidance counselors, and, truthfully, I don't blame them.

See, I am loud -and critical - about how they - and most parents, and kids, for that matter, pick colleges.

I think they are 100% wrong in their approach.

As a side note, I can't blame them. The problem is the SYSTEM. The national average ratio of students to counselors is 400:1.

In private high schools, the ratio is much better, but guidance counselors lack training on career development, financial aid/scholarships and a host of other areas you'd hope they would cover.

Back to the main point: in my opinion, there is WAAAAAAY too much emphasis on the *four* years of college...

...but NOT the 40 or 50 *post-college* years!

Think about it. The reason to go to college is, ostensibly, to prepare for live AFTER college, five or six years hence.

But here's one problem: who the H-E-double-hockey sticks knows what the hot jobs will be in that time?

Put another way, do you know anyone who predicted that Uber would be a multi-billion company five years ago? Lyft? Pinterest?

Or that Air BnB would have a market capitalization greater than Hilton, without owning any real estate (and giving Hilton a 100 year head start in the hotel business?)

These companies barely existed (or didn't exist) five years ago. Now they are dominant in their industries!

It's terribly easy to go to college and major in NOTHING that an employer values.

Women's Studies?

Puppetry? (No joke, that's a real major at UCONN and many colleges)

Speaking of jokes, the situation facing our kids is not funny - it's as serious as cancer:

- 80% of kids change majors, prolonging the college years at $70K per year

- 50% of college grads don't have a job that requires a college degree....TWO YEARS after graduating

- Student debt passed the 1.5Trillion mark, and defaults rise every time they're reported, it seems.

Here's the point:

If you don't plan...

If you decide to "WING IT," you're setting yourself up to fail.

The next few chapters deal with The Next 40.

CHAPTER 10

WHAT SHOULD COLLEGE PREPARE YOU FOR, ANYWAY?

Thanks to skyrocketing college costs and a lousy job market, this question is on the frontal lobes of many parents' brains.

Some argue that college should prepare you to get a good job.

While I completely understand and empathize with this thought, I don't agree.

College is not a trade school. But it is a place that ostensibly prepares young adults for adulthood.

So let's look at what will be needed to succeed when your child graduates. We don't have a crystal ball, so the logical strategy should be to learn how to deal with NEW situations that don't come with a manual or textbook.

Take mathematics, as an example. There is only one right answer, you either solve the equation or you don't.

But in life, there could be five "right" answers, because life isn't a math problem. College is supposed to help you for life, *ergo*[11] college should help you learn to navigate a set of ambiguous facts.

This isn't my opinion only. Surveys of CEO's and other executives who make hiring decisions almost always point to "critical

---

[11] I took Latin in high school and really use words and phrases like *"ergo" ad nauseum"* and *"Inter alia"* whenever I can, to please the ladies.

thinking"[12] and innovation skills as the most highly desired characteristics they want from employees.

Why? Because you need skills to cope with situations where there's no one right answer. Can you hone critical thinking and creative thinking skills in college?

Sure, by experimenting, failing and starting again. By debating ideas and solutions to problems. And by advocating your positions, arguing, cajoling, selling to other critical thinkers.

But if, during college, you spend most of your class time taking standardized, "fill in the bubble" tests where you regurgitate facts and get graded by teaching assistants or other non-tenure-track professors, how much will you improve your critical thinking skills?

On the other hand, if you take classes with Ph.D professors, who encourage class participation and challenge students to articulate their ideas on paper and verbally, do you think your critical thinking skills stand a better chance of improving?

The book *Academically Adrift* by Arum and Roksa discuss how little college students actually learn while in college, measured by a little-known test called the Collegiate Learning Assessment Test.

Never heard of it? Maybe the reason has something to do with the fact that almost half of all students show zero improvement in critical thinking skills after two years of college, and more than a third do not improve after four years!

Arum and Roksa's sequel book, *Aspiring Adults Adrift* is also a must read, making a strong case that those college graduates with advanced critical thinking skills are employed in greater numbers in satisfactory jobs.

If you haven't figured it out, this chapter is a strong argument for a liberal arts education. According to *Academically Adrift*, some

---

[12] Waaaaaay overused buzzword, almost as bad as "passion."

majors promote the advancement of critical thinking skills better than others, such as STEM (Science, Technology, Engineering and Math) - no surprise.

But also: English, History and Philosophy.

Now you might be thinking, when's the last time you heard of an employer grabbing the phone and shouting, "Get me the philosophy major! I need someone to think for me!," but the thinking is the new liberal art.

In my mind, the best of both worlds is a critical thinking major AND strategic internships along the way that help develop workplace-ready skills.

RESOURCE: **www.CollegeAdmissionsWebcast.com** has information about what employers of the future are looking for in employees, how choose a major that prepares you for a real job that actually exists and other important, valuable information.

CHAPTER 11

WHAT SHOULD I MAJOR IN?

**Read this chapter to figure out what the hell you want to do
with the rest of your life**

"I've always wanted to be a paleo-neuro-nano-forensic speech
pathologist since I was five."

When 16 year old kids look me in the eye and earnestly declare that
they know exactly how they want to spend the next 40 years of their
lives (after their four years of college), I try to suppress a chuckle.

Yes, I believe that a percentage - a miniscule percentage - of kids
have pretty much always known what they want to do with the rest
of their lives. But most 16 year olds do not, and cannot. (Ditto for
many 50 year olds!)

When someone tells me that they want to be a lawyer, for example,
I'll ask a few questions, such as:

- How did you arrive at that interest? (If they're honest,
  they'll admit it's from watching Law and Order, or because
  their cousin went to law school)

- Do you know anyone who is an attorney?

- Have you ever interned or "shadowed" an attorney so you
  can see what they do all day? (In the off-chance that reality
  is different than *Law and Order* or *The Good Wife*.)

Even if someone is dead certain on their career, keep in mind that a
huge percentage (50-80%, depending on which study you believe)
of kids change their majors. Whatever the statistics, there's a very
good chance that a college student will change his major at least
once.

One of the biggest problems relating to switching majors is that you could prolong your college career, which means:

- Spending more on tuition at $50,000 per year (or more), and

- The opportunity cost of delaying entrance into the job force, perhaps another $50,000 per year.

So if you take two extra years to get out of school, you could be committing a $200,000 error. Yowza.

Not to mention the uncertainty and emotional, existential angst surrounding the *What should I do with the rest of my life?* question.

(Note: This is not a book on feelings. I don't have feelings - ask Pearl. Watch Dr. Phil or something.)

Plenty of CEO and CEO-types who are in a position to hire people will tell you that they don't care what you majored in. They want you to be able to think on your feet, deal with ambiguous situations where there may be more than right answer, work independently, take initiative to figure things out on your own, and possess other similar, related qualities.

Still, I think it's a good idea to think about careers while you're in high school. The more time a 16 or 17 year old can devote to thinking about what she wants things to look like in five years, the easier it is to "backward plan" what it's going to take to get there.

In other words, if a high school senior has a reasonable idea that he is interested in two or three (hopefully) overlapping careers, then he has a new context to evaluate every choice presented to him over the next four years.

Every decision he makes will have at least indirect - or direct - implications on his reality five years hence.

So how does a 16 or 17 year old kid decide what the hell he wants to do with the rest of his life?

I'm no career expert, and don't really take stock in most advice I hear, such as "Find your passion!"

Irritating! C'mon. A person's passion and their ability to earn a living are not necessarily the same thing, at least in real life. Plenty of people lead rewarding, fulfilling lives, like what they do for a living, but don't necessarily have a "passion" for their jobs.

Disclaimer: Approximately four years ago, our firm partnered with a top career counseling firm to help high school kids learn how they're "wired," what they should consider as majors (and what they should stay away from!) and whether their chosen field is in growth mode or in decline, and other important issues.

If you're attempting to tackle this on your own, I recommend using Naviance, the web-based college planning software used by most high school guidance departments. (If you're unsure whether your school has a subscription, ask your guidance counselor.)

Most kids think of Naviance as a program that handicaps their chances of admission: you plug in your GPA and SAT or ACT scores, a list of schools, and Naviance produces a nice graph ("Scattergram,") that compares your information versus other kids from your high school who got into the colleges on your list over the past three or more years.

(I'm a fan of Naviance, but I'll readily admit that I do not use it because it's limited. Every admissions officer will tell you that they consider more than a dozen factors beyond grades and scores: awards or recognition received, extra-curricular activities like sports and volunteer hours, recommendations, ethnicity and geographic diversity, to name a few. And you're not only competing with kids from your high school - you're going up against applicants from all over the world! I use another, private software that quantifies all of these considerations, and more. See https://www.lockwoodcollegeprep.com/inner-circle-sneak-preview if you are interested.)

One overlooked or underutilized feature of Naviance that is the career and emotional intelligence modules.

There are two, roughly 25 minute exercises in Naviance that address these areas. The emotional intelligence exercise is called Do What You Are or something cheesy like that.

Notwithstanding the goofy name, almost all of the kids I know who have done this exercise report that the results - the description of their personality - are usually accurate.

While not failsafe, this exercise can help a gregarious, outgoing, shucking and jiving kind of kid avoid a career like accounting, that will stick him in a cubicle like Dilbert.

The career assessment exercise is also worthwhile, if you can get past some of the nutty suggestions ("Astronaut," "Park Attendant")[13] that distract kids.

Remember, it's a software, not a real, live career expert making suggestions. Try to look at the reasons why astronaut was suggested.

Was it because you're task oriented, able to work without direct, hovering supervision and enjoy challenges and taking risks?

Quick story about one of our clients, Isabel. We put Isabel through our career counseling service to help her figure out her career path. She was very interested in architecture, in fact she had interned at a local firm and had even taken a course over the summer at a college.

When she did our strength finding assessment (The "Birkman"), architecture correlated very highly with her values, strengths and how she was wired as a person. But there was a catch:

The Bureau of Labor Statistics shows that architecture is one of the WORST fields to get into today!

---

[13] Wish I was kidding.

So we encouraged Isabel to consider other fields that also matched up closely with her profile, such as urban planning and civil engineering.

This is how you prevent graduating with a degree that prepares you for a non-existent job!

Does every student come away knowing exactly what she wants to do with the next 40 years of her life? Of course not.

At the end of the day, it's a major victory to head to college with three-to-four careers in mind. But you'll get this clarity only if you put in the time and effort - with the right tools - that this exploration deserves.

CHAPTER 12

THE SECOND BEST TIME FOR KIDS TO GET SERIOUS ABOUT COLLEGE PLANNING

(The best time is in utero.)

Also, what to do if your child has not taken Princeton Review since age 4 and isn't conversant in Mandarin or Warlpiri (look it up, I did)

Question: Why should you hire a college consultant for your 5th grader?

Answer: Because your neighbor with a fourth grader did.

I'll confess that I have a handful of 9th graders in my practice. Because I was more of a slacker growing up, I have a hard time relating to the parents, but I see where they're coming from. The moment you set foot in high school, you're creating a body of work that admissions officers will scrutinize.

When you apply to college, you're writing up your Closing Argument, by way of your applications and essays, highlighting that body of work that commenced in 9th grade.

By the way, this is one of my biggest pet peeves about high school guidance departments, most don't have the Big College Meeting with kids and families until 11th grade, or at a point when almost half the college body of work has been created.

Putting my hangups aside, let's examine the college admissions process from my slightly off, non-mainstream "marketing perspective." Consider these three points:

1. Having a resume that features a handful of "Atypical Teen Activities" (special stuff that most kids don't even think about doing) will answer decidedly the core question asked by every admissions officer when they review each application: *Why should we take YOU instead of any these 5,000 other kids with the same grades and standardized test scores?*[14]

2. The Junior year is the most critical year of the "body of work" you'll present to the college: grades, scores and extracurricular involvement.

3. I said it before and I'll say it again: the time to plan your Junior year is NOT after it's started (that's not planning, it's called "reacting")...it's BEFORE 11th grade.

If you have done nothing interesting in 9th and 10th grades, then all of a sudden join six clubs in 11th grade, you won't be fooling anyone. Your resume will signal to the admissions committee that you loaded up on activities only to look good for college.

In other words, you have a bad case of BAJ (Born Again Junior phenomenon).

If you have no history of volunteering or participating in anything in 9th and 10th grades, it may not be that convincing for your mom to put together a three-on-three basketball tournament that will raise money to simultaneously wipe out:

- Breast cancer

- Autism

- Mom's with breast cancer and autism

- Chron's Disease

---

[14] Technically, that question does not appear anywhere on the college applications, but it is THE QUESTION.

- Colitis

- A disease to be named later

But the fact is that, the earlier you plan, the more options you'll have.

~ Cliche Alert ~

If you fail to plan, you plan to fail!

(I don't care if that's cheesy, it's true.)

You may find what I'm about to say to be contradictory, but I feel it's necessary: I don't really like the thought of "packaging" kids for college, which is ironic[15] given my chosen field.

However, if we've learned nothing from recent events, including the Harvard lawsuit brought by a Chinese-American student who was not admitted despite superior academic credentials, college admissions is only PARTIALLY a meritocracy, at best.

For many students, it's more about marketing than a meritocracy.

I don't like this, but that's just how it works, here on Planet Earth. I have chosen to deal with reality, as opposed to living in the Land of Shoulds.[16]

Final thought: whether or not YOU are on board, the college "train" keeps chugging along, inevitably, month after month, week after week. Even if you're not mentally"ready" for the train to arrive and depart.

The later you start, the fewer options you have.

---

[15] Not "hypocritical," of course!

[16] Pearl Lockwood gets credit for that one!

RESOURCE: Want more information about how to "market" yourself to college? Head on over to www.CollegeAdmissionsWebcast.com.

CHAPTER 13

ADVICE FOR "HELICOPTER" PARENTS

STOP!

CHAPTER 14

ADVICE FOR "SNOWPLOW PARENTS"

See previous chapter.

CHAPTER 15

THE PROBLEM WITH HELICOPTERING/SNOWPLOWING

A few years ago, long before the Felicity-Lori college scandal, I was sitting in my office with client, who owns a local advertising agency. He had arrived a few minutes late.

"How ya doin', Paul," I asked.

"Aren't you going to ask me why I was late?" Paul inquired.

"Um, OK - how come?" I replied, noticing his half-smile.

"I was interviewing someone for a job as a graphic designer…" he said.

"OK…" I said.

Pause.

"Don't you want to know how the interview went?" Paul asked, leaning forward, now sporting a full-blown smirk.

"Actually, I wasn't going to ask, but, yes, tell me,"I said.

"For the applicant…or for his mother?" Paul said.

"Are you [expletive deleted] kidding me? His MOMMY showed up!?" I couldn't believe it.

"Yep. The sad thing is that this is NOT the first time this happened," he said, shaking his head.

I have since heard of dozens of similar examples of parents accompanying (not dropping off!) their kids on job interviews, asking questions of the interviewer, calling after to follow up and so on.

You may be rolling your eyes, saying God, that's ridiculous - who would ever do that?

OK, maybe not, now that we know lengths celebrities and ultra rich will go to snowplow all obstacles out of the way of their children.

We all do this, to some degree or another. It's a natural instinct, hard wired into our DNA, I suppose.[17]

Pearl and I have four kids, two boys and two girls, 8th grade through sophomore in college. Even if we wanted to, we could not possibly do their homework for them. Between games and practices, rehearsals and plays and our work obligations, it's a major challenge to get them to show up to these activities at all, let alone on time.

But we feel guilty when one of the kids underperforms. OK, Pearl feels guilty. I don't (but I'm supportive of her, so it's like I'm guilty.)

She feels badly because she can't spend time with them on homework the way she thinks other parents do, or that we haven't invested in expensive tutors and specialists like many of our family and friends.

Pearl had developed a cute little ritual. First, she logs onto the parent "Portal" at 4:50 am (online access to grades is a dangerous addiction that needs a support group) then scowls, proclaiming loudly, "[Child Name] has a [unprintable] D in math!"

I'm up now.

Next, she fumes about our kid not trying, not going to extra help, that we need to hire a tutor but they're so expensive, someday this will catch up to him and other comments in similar vein.

---

[17] Easy, Lockwood, this is a college admissions book, not an anthropology book.

114

At 6:45, sleepy-eyed [Child] is summoned before her. Pearl is judge, jury and executioner.

He's read the riot act, ripped a new orifice and asked what the hell he was thinking.

I'm asked to offer my two cents, which is always in complete agreement (do you think I'm stupid?). Then we ask for an explanation.

[Child's] response is some version of a blank, downward stare. Perhaps a few mumbled, never satisfactory, words. Then we take away XBox, or the laptop, or phone, all three or some combination.

Next, there's a temporary improvement in behavior, such as the bed being made without asking for up to two consecutive days, getting up for school by using an alarm (not Mommy or Daddy), visible evidence of studying (i.e. open books on the desk).

To me, it's self-evident that this doesn't work, because we've seen this short-lived pattern dozens of times.

But Pearl is not as fatalistic. How are we going to motivate this kid? She wonders.

That is the wrong question.

I don't think you CAN motivate a kid, or anyone. And punishment doesn't change behavior. Don't get me wrong - I DO punish him, by taking away XBox, the phone, or other equivalent.

I suspect that all this does is make me feel vaguely satisfied, as though there's justice in our house. And I feel good that I'm doing something, instead of rewarding bad behavior.

Then I tell myself that it's good for our other kids to see that we won't condone this behavior.

We also reward for good behavior, like buying ice cream and other small acknowledgements of a job well done.

But I don't think that he - or most kids - are truly motivated by these gimmicks. Instead,

I feel like the desire to achieve has to come from within, tied to the joy and satisfaction of mastering difficult tasks. (Read *Drive* by Dan Pink.)

In other words, this kid has got to be self-motivated. I'll tell Pearl, We can't want it more than he does.

To her credit, instead of throwing something at me, she usually agrees.

But I understand her, and to an extent, my impulse to want to do stuff for our son (["Child"] is never one of our girls of course!).

We birthed them, diapered them, fed them, stayed up at night with them and the whole drill. A natural extension is hiring tutors, doing 95% of their school project and working with private coaches for each sport they play. It makes sense that we'd want to be there for every step thereafter. I get that.

But our job as parents is to prepare our kids to be independent members of society. There's no two ways about it - it's a disservice to be that Helicopter Parent, or to create a structure or system that encourages dependence on tutors, coaches or any outsider. (By the way, one of my biggest gripes with K-12 schooling is that it's designed to prevent kids from growing up. But that's another topic.)

Helicoptering retards our kids' growth in the not-so-long long run. If you think I'm being harsh, just imagine what things will be like immediately after high school. College professors take kindly to parental intervention. They're tenured, and immune to a lot of the crap parents may have heaped on teachers and school principals along the way.).

Of course it's ok to help your kid out. This means scheduling and organizing things for them, and other low level tasks.

It does not mean writing their college essays or putting resumes together.

If you really want your child to be successful, fight your helicopter impulse!

CHAPTER 16

HOW TO SABOTAGE YOUR CHILDREN

Following are excerpts from an edited transcript of a PRE-scandal discussion Pearl and I had on our show, *College Talk Tuesday* (Tuesdays 12:00pm, www.CollegeTalkTuesday.live). We chatted about some case studies where parents shot themselves in the collective feetsies. This was so good (I'm talking about Pearl's stuff) that I had to put it in this book. Valuable lessons, and perhaps a little cringy and eye-roll-inducing!

Andy: All righty. Welcome to *College Talk Tuesday*. Pearl and Andy Lockwood here from Lockwood College Prep. Hello. Hello to you, my bride and partner.

Pearl: Hello, Andy. My groom and partner. Hello, everybody.

Andy: Partner as in the business partner sense, not in the politically correct life partner sense?

Pearl: I think we fall under life partner as well. You're still my life partner even though you are a traditional husband to me. You're still considered my life partner.

Andy: Do you consider it an equal partnership?

Pearl: I do.

Andy: Are you more like the general partner and I'm like a limited partner?

Pearl: No. I see us both as equal partners.

Andy: Okay. Well, we've gotten that out of the way, which is very important.

Pearl: Sure you're all interested.

Andy: Our show is really about helping parents and kids navigate the whole college process. Getting into college, paying for college...AND avoiding deadly mistakes, which is what we're going to be talking about now. We're gonna be talking about an amalgam of a couple of actual clients who are managing to sabotage themselves in a more extreme way than most parents, including you hopefully.

I think it's instructive because of the psychology involved. We talk about this all the time. We always say we don't judge. I think in this case we're judging a little bit. I just want you to know that we're telling you this, not really as much for amusement purposes, but really, also, for instructive purposes. Fair to say?

Pearl: Yes, absolutely. This is a great examples, including one where a parent hired us and then decided to do nothing.

Andy: Do nothing?

Pearl: Yes, that's an active choice. In a strange way, it's opposite of being active but it has a consequence too.

Andy: "Doing nothing" doesn't come close to describing this particular situation.. We have to be a little nimble here in terms of not revealing too much or betraying confidences. Let's say that they live in Connecticut. They are a very nice couple. Just from the get-go, however, we knew that there was gonna be some issues.

This is now a couple years ago. Their kid was very smart, he applied to a whole bunch of elite northeastern liberal arts colleges. Some of which give need-based money. Some which give merit-based money.

Andy: He ended up getting into a great college - his top choice school - that offers a lot of need-based money, but no merit-based money.

The issue was they had retained us, specifically Pearl, to advise them and file the financial aid forms for them. This is again, going back two years. But they never actually filed the forms! Describe what happened.

Pearl: Well, a couple of years ago?

Andy: Yeah.

Pearl: Okay. A couple of years ago, this was when the student was applying right for the first time to schools.

Pearl: The issue was the assets. Okay. There were assets that were part of litigation. There was a hope I guess that there was gonna be a resolution before the deadline to file, but there wasn't. There was a lot of inertia and waiting and waiting, followed by more waiting and waiting. I'd ask, *Well, can we file the forms? Can you give me what you have right now?* Radio silence. Crickets. Crickets!

Andy: Silly thing to me is that because you file with whatever you have in this "pot" at the time. In this case, it was a trust where our client was being accused of doing something untoward. Again, we don't judge. Our recommendation was that, because this money was subject to this controversy, these assets would NOT go on the financial aid forms because other people have a claim on them.

Andy: What you (Pearl) recommended is what I recommended, in my numerous, separate conversations and emails, with the clients (probably 30 exchanges between you, me and them), was just go ahead and file it as if you don't have those assets in your possession.

Certainly, you cannot use them as a resource to be able to pay for college, which is what the spirit of the regulations are about.

Instead, there's back and forth between them and us. *Well, I don't know, should we?*. Plus, just general back and forth, *I don't know if he should apply there or not. What do you think?* A lot of-

Pearl: Questioning and over questioning. What if this? What if that? What if this? What if that? What if, what if, what if, what if. Okay. What if the world ends?

121

Andy: Can't get out of their own way. That was the overwhelming response that you and I had each had individually.

Pearl: It's like the stress of the college planning has a tipping point. They passed it. That took over.

Took over so much that almost I have to call it insanity. It was an insanity that took over. That inertia.

And where their kid did everything right! He worked his butt off for the four years. Had good grades and the scores got his essays in on time. But his parents just waited and waited. They hired us, that was a start.

Andy: Just so you see we know what we're talking about. They retained us to help with the applications and the essays, as well as apply for financial aid.

But at the end of the day, when it was time to implement our advice, they just couldn't pull the trigger and file based on the facts we were working with at the time.

Look, if their lawsuit gets resolved a different way, in favor of our client, then we could amend the FAFSA and CSS Profile.

And if it doesn't get resolved that way then there's no harm no foul. But they never filed.

Then...the kid gets into this school that he deserves and is dying to go to. It turns out there's no financial aid available because he never applied! And now the mom is freaked out about the expense!

Pearl: Right. It's ridiculous. Nothing was available because they didn't apply! Not even loans. If you want to mitigate your out-of-pocket expense in the first year of college, you have to apply!

Andy: Then the mom sends us emails and phone calls every few days, bemoaning, "Oh, I wish we never did this. Do you think we can not accept the early decision? Can we try and negotiate?"

Pearl: These are happening as the kid is literally headed to college. It's August. He's matriculated.

Andy: She's still second guessing it even after he's there. *We can't afford to pay this.* Then she asks about transferring...

Pearl: I say, *Let me submit the forms still. Take a loan,* just to get by.

Andy: The dad, incidentally, is very well versed in finances.

Pearl: He's a professional CPA.

Andy: So it wasn't an ignorance thing. They're in fact, they're too smart - maybe that's the problem.

Pearl: They fought the whole thing. They just were paralyzed.

Andy: I don't remember what the reasons were for not filing, other than this legal stuff up in the air and being too distracted.

Pearl: The up in the air stuff was too distracting. Then they had a loss in the family. A normal course of life event, loss. Immediately, subsequently after, I told them, AGAIN, that I can still file the forms for last year. They'll be able to get loans at the very least, but they won't be considered for anything else.

Andy: Well, wait a minute - this morning, you told me that finally, you looked at what they would've qualified for and it was potentially $20,000 to $30,000 that they left on the table.

Pearl: Yes! Turns out that they actually would have qualified last year - IF WE HAD FILED!

Andy: Oh my god. Even with all this mess.

Pearl: Even with the mess. Even with all the assets.

So next, they tell me, "Well, now we don't have the money to pay for the second year." The mother is insisting the kid transfer. But he loves the school. He is succeeding - he's kicking butt. It's a tragedy. I mean, it's really very sad.

Andy: From his perspective, he must have thought *Why'd you even let me apply here if you're telling me that we can't afford it! We should of at least had a discussion about it.*

Pearl: It's unconscionable. Anyway, moving right along. We're at a point now where they certainly want now not to make that mistake again. So the mother is continually talking to me about the kid transferring to a cheaper school. But of course, the kid doesn't want to transfer. He has not filed or filled out one application for transfer. Keep in mind, the transfer applications, and financial aid applications, have deadlines too.

Andy: It's two versus one. The mom now wants them to transfer and the dad and the son are not interested at all in the kid going anywhere else.

Pearl: I'm trying to corral them all back in to get on the same page, because I don't want to prepare financial aid forms for a bunch of colleges that the kid isn't even applying to!

Andy: There's a whole other thing, too - at this point, the mom apparently dropped off the face of the earth. Who knows where she went?

Pearl: Anyhow….I continually urge them to get their forms in. Stop talking about it. Get them in. See what they say. You're assuming you'll get a "No" before you even try. The only promise I can make every one of you is that, if you do not file your financial aid forms you're not getting anything.

Andy: You could get merit.

Pearl: You could get some merit if the college doesn't require you to file financial aid forms. You could that's true. In this case-

Andy: You seem very aggressive and angry.

Pearl: It's a shame for this kid. My heart goes out to him. He really did all the right things. This is a real travesty.

Andy: That's the collateral damage (of parent analysis paralysis).

Pearl: Right. It's very sad. He kept up his end of the bargain. Anyway, the real crime in this is finally yesterday, I filed last year's forms and this year's using 2016 and 2017.

Andy: Tax returns.

Pearl: Yes. To file with the assets as they are and were and now. Whatever, it doesn't even matter. The point is, after all this, we learned the kid did qualify for some need-based aid.

Andy: At least 20,000 to 30,000 of free money.

Pearl: Right. It's so upsetting I just can't get over it.

Andy: It's still weird to us, even though we've seen everything. We've been in this field for 18 plus years Psychology is just as important as the logical aspects of what we do and I think all-

Pearl: It's not just the college prep, right? All the college prep in the world wouldn't have avoided this.

Andy: We see all kinds of things that crop up. There are obstacles that are self-imposed in many ways for all of us, present company included!

You described a flagrant egregious example of parents that couldn't get out of their own way. They had the best intentions. They were referred by another great client of ours with a warning. Little did I know! I thought she was kidding when she told me, "There's gonna be some stuff."

Andy: So far, there's no damage that we can perceive, although we don't really know. If he's forced to transfer or just the fact that he's got this going on in his background. Who knows what kind of therapy he'll need. Truthfully, it's amazing to me that he can compartmentalize this and still get great grades, with all the nutty parent stuff in the background. Who knows what the conversations are behind the scenes. The takeaway here is not just to-

Pearl: Air out our gripes.

Andy: I wouldn't even call it a gripe. I think this is not really a clinical type of show, although today it feels like it!

We usually talk about tips for parents and kids, i.e. what they need to do.

But the takeaway is not only to think about what you SHOULD be doing, but also, what are you NOT doing? Inaction has the effect of hamstringing you or sabotaging your ability to get into a top school. Or to pay for a top school like qualifying for scholarships and financial aid. We see all kinds of examples of people sticking their heads in the sand, knowing that this whole process is happening but refusing to participate.

Andy: It could mean hiring someone to help you, but it doesn't always mean that. A lot of people are so overwhelmed by this process, because it's really confusing. It's not the way it was 30 years ago. They need some type of help. If you do retain someone like Pearl to help you, don't blow off all their advice, requests for information, etc.. Don't think somehow, magically, this process is going to happen itself without participating or making decisions.

Andy: Another self-sabotage example we spoke about off the air, involved a very successful parent who made millions of dollars. Now he's unemployed, which is another discussion. My point is that this self-sabotage discussion pertains even to people who, on the surface, are very successful by any objective measurement. Even those guys can be just flat out the right word is-

Pearl: Careless. Sloppy. Inattentive.

Andy: Yes. Inattentive. Or they just make you scratch your head with their indecision or lack of responsiveness.

Pearl: We warn you there's a lot of balls up in the air in this process.

Andy: It's not an intelligence thing. It's not a success thing. In the second-

Pearl: It's psychological. It really is.

Andy: Of course, it is. In the second case, they're having their son apply to 30 schools, including every Ivy League school. He doesn't have a snowball's chance in hell of getting in. He's gonna be writing essay after essay after essay and just stressing out. Being harassed by his parents.

Pearl: As if that's going to further his chances of getting in. I mean, it's almost like there's this exercise in futility. Well, I tried.

Andy: That what I was getting at is that-

Pearl: It's not the right effort.

Andy: That's what they're focusing on the impossible dream, as opposed to the easy stuff, which is what you're asking them to do. In other words, hiring someone for their advice, and then ignoring it entirely. That to me seems one of the silliest things to do.

Again, I'm not judging because there's examples in our own personal lives. For example, I know what it takes to drop 20 pounds, but I'm not always doing it! I have an accountant who gives me advice to do this and that. I take some of it and I discard the rest of it. I'm not bemoaning it or second guessing myself or blaming others. It's just that I wanna have a clear conscience with my decisions.

Pearl: To sleep at night.

Andy: Hopefully, you found these stories educational and maybe you Hopefully, feel better about yourself! Very few people, in our experience, are of *this* caught up. The point is that-

Pearl: It's birthed from neuroses.

Andy: Maybe. I don't know what it is. The point is that this process the whole college process especially from eleventh grade until you throw in your applications hopefully fall of senior year. It's going to happen, whether or not you are "up for it."

It's like a train that comes into Penn Station at a certain time, and it leaves at a certain time. It doesn't care if you're ready for it, or if

you're second-guessing the schedule or whatever it just happens. Either you're onboard the train or you're not onboard the train.

Pearl: Running to catch a train when it's already leaving the station is very, very stressful as you can imagine. I don't recommend doing it that way.

Andy: The woman we were talking about was trying to get the kid on another train while he was already on the right one!

Pearl: The kid was already matriculated, and she was asking me, "Can we go back to the schools he got admitted to last year and see if we can still go?" No.

Andy: We gave two different examples but they have commonality.

Pearl: I'm now thinking of a third. Of a student and/or the parent really sees them (way up) here academically-

Andy: Oh, that's so common.

Pearl: They're going early decision to the pie-in-the-sky college. Disregarding other deadlines. Then, the student gets denied in December, which gets us into reality, and mad dash to more realistic schools.

Andy: Yes, it's because what they were banking on didn't happen - they didn't get into Princeton or whatever. Then all of a sudden, it's like, "Oh my God! What do we do now?" Panic!!!!

To be clear, we NEVER say, "don't apply to Princeton." But we do say, make sure you execute Plan B, Plan C just in case the Hail Mary doesn't pan out, so you won't have to do this mad dash.

Pearl: Right. It may be painful to realize that you may not get into where you see yourself deserving, or where your parents want you to go. Again, bemoaning that and NOT making a plan B is to your detriment.

Andy: People make their own realities. There's all this talk about alternative facts and fake news and whatever.

Pearl: Everyone does it.

Andy: Whatever you call it, we all interpret things a certain way, that may or may not be the same as other people. The danger is when you're not open to rational input from other sources and you just have your blinders on, ignoring other possibilities.

Pearl: It affects your life choices.

Andy: It affects your near term and your medium to long-term life also. It's a lot better to go through the short-term discomfort of throwing in a few other applications or digging up paperwork. That short-term discomfort avoids some severe, excruciating medium term to long-term pain.

Pearl: OK, please share this just so you can loop in other parents who need to know this information. If you want them to know. Okay. All right. Should we sign off now?

Andy: Yeah.

Pearl: All right. Thanks a lot for watching.

Andy: Have a good week.

Pearl: We'll be back with College Talk Tuesday next week.

CHAPTER 17

WHAT YOU'RE REALLY DOING WHEN YOU FILL OUT A COLLEGE APPLICATION

You may think you're filling out a tiresome, annoying application, but you're actually answering a question:

Why should we take you, compared to these other 5,000 kids with the same grades and test scores?

In other words, What makes you different? What is your "USP" (Unique Selling Proposition, a marketing term)?

How would you answer that?

I'm very active in my community.

I'm hard working.

I'm well-rounded.

I made National Honor Society.

I'm a leader.

People really, really like me! (Yawn.)

Question: do any of these answers seem UNIQUE?

Were you an admissions officer, would you latch onto any of those responses and say, Eureka! A hard-working, community-oriented leader! Finally!

Hmm, how do I put this gently....

WHAT PLANET ARE YOU FROM?

Before I tell you how to answer this question, let's pull back and look at the landscape.

There are approximately 28,000 high schools in America. That means that there are at least 28,000 valedictorians.

Actually, there are thousands more, because many high schools have co-valedictorians.

Manhasset High School, on the North Shore of Long Island, had four for the class of 2012! I imagine this is because it's a special district, full of gifted, wonderful children!

I'm picking on this particular school district, but making fun of affluent areas is like shooting fish in a teeny-weeny barrel. Other examples:

Jericho High School inducted one of my clients into the National Honor Society... her and about 189 other deserving students, out of approximately 230 students. As my client put it, It would have been easier to count the kids that DIDN'T make it!

We have it on authority (double-secret source) that teachers at a certain affluent district are not permitted to give grades lower than a B.

Back to the stats: so there maybe 30,000-something valedictorians and a similar amount of salutatorians in the country.

Newsflash: they don't all get into Harvard, Duke, etc.!

In fact, thousands of them are rejected, often at the expense of lower-ranked, "lesser" candidates who are admitted "over" them.

Why?

Because these kids were atypical.

Sure, a percentage of admits at most competitive schools fall into special categories that you may not, such as:

- Minorities

- Legacies

- Recruited athletes

- "Development" cases (described below)

- International students

- Children of professors at that college

Sidebar: Ever wonder what's behind the explosive growth of international students? Here's a quick factoid: colleges are recruiting overseas. Brown University has an office in Mumbai. In 2010, Brown enrolled 249 Mumbaian undergraduates. (Mumbaian should be a word.) In 2005, they had 98.

These "hooks" take up a majority (almost two-thirds of many top schools, according to Admissions Confidential, by Rachel Toor, former admissions officer at Duke.)

Another former admissions officer at a competitive colleges estimated that 25% of the incoming class of his college were admitted for academic reasons only, according to *College Unranked* by Lloyd Thacker.

So it's important to understand your odds if you don't have one of the aforementioned four "hooks."

How to you make your application stand out? I call this the CASA Approach.© CASA stands for:

Consistent

Atypical

Strategic

Activities

If there existed a "magic formula" for admissions to top colleges for the "normal" kid, this is it. (There isn't, otherwise this book would be a lot more expensive!). Here are the elements of our approach:

"Consistent" means that you don't wait until the last minute to pad your resume with a mish-mosh of unrelated extra-curricular activities. Sophomore year is great, Junior year is more challenging, by Senior year it's too late.

So if you're reading this in your Senior year of high school, and your resume is a little thin, don't rush out and join five clubs, because it won't matter.

But if you're a Sophomore, time is your friend. If a Junior, you may still have enough time to employ this strategy.

"Consistent" also means that, if you've played an instrument or engaged in another activity for three years, but drop it the fourth, it will raise a red flag to an admissions officer. She'll want to know what happened.

Are there good reasons for dropping an activity? Yes, such as you had to make room in your schedule for something important (an internship, working, religious commitment, etc.)

Not that you just lost interest.

"Atypical" is important. "ATA's" (Atypical Teen Activities) stand for the idea that you should not just do the same things that your friends or peers do if you want to stand out on a college application.

"Strategic" means that you have an overarching plan, a strategy that provides the framework for your ATA's.

A common way this concept plays out is when a student is interested in a particular field, say health care.

When I started working with Monique (not her real name), in the beginning of her Junior year, she had a vague idea that she might want to be a nurse or doctor.

Monique (still not her real name) was a high achieving kid from an affluent neighborhood in Long Island's Suffolk County. Like many of her peers, she was involved with a handful of extra-curricular activities: student government, debate club, Girl Scouts and a few others. Not to mention a bunch of AP classes, SAT and ACT review sessions, the whole gamut.

In other words, a BRWK ("Bright Well-rounded Kid" in admissions-speak).

I, of course, suggested that Monique take on another activity (because sleeping is overrated!) - "shadowing" a nurse or doctor.

(I did not recommend a full-blown internship for Monique, as this would have been too time consuming and would melt her brain if I breathed a word about it.)

I asked Monique if any of her friends were doing something along the lines of what I suggested. They weren't.

That's exactly why YOU should! I exclaimed.

Here's what happened.

CHAPTER 18

GIRL GETS $611,600 IN SCHOLARSHIPS

As I was midway through the first draft of this book, I had an unusual conversation with Monique's mom.

In her Senior year, Monique was admitted to 10 of the 10 colleges she applied to, receiving $152,900 of scholarships ($611,600 over four years, provided that she maintains a minimum satisfactory GPA). Not too shabby!

Monique was a very good, but not elite, student.

Her SAT's were strong, but by no means off the charts.

Monique applied to competitive, 2nd tier colleges - not Ivy League or equivalent.

Monique is NOT an underrepresented minority.

Monique's family makes about $500K per year.

This may be the most interesting part of the story: Mom told me that many of Monique's soccer teammates, who had the same or better grades and scores, were rejected or waitlisted by several of the same schools.

As they bemoaned this year's admissions results, Monique's mom kept her mouth shut, not wanting to rub it in.

I asked "What do you think the difference was between Monique and the other girls with the same grades and scores" (how serving was THAT?)?

I knew the answer. :)

Mom reminded me that, back in Monique's Junior year, I had pressured her (nicely!) into interning at a local hospital.

Her objection: none of her peers was doing anything like this. Monique questioned whether she should be spending her time this way.

My answer: "That's EXACTLY why you should be doing it! It will stand out on your resume - it's ATYPICAL!"

A week later, she landed an internship.

Two months later, three days into her new experience, I asked her, casually, how it was going.

"I'm so happy! This is TOTALLY what I want to do with the rest of my life!" She yelled.

"But do you like it?" I asked. (That's why I get paid the big bucks.)

Once it ended, she added two more mini-internships over the summer and fall.

The good news was that the internships solidified Monique's choice of career.

The great news was that this helped Monique stand out to the colleges on her list, get in, and get all those juicy scholarships!

Yatzee.

RESOURCE: Learn how to multiply your chances of getting a ton of fat, juicy scholarships at www.CollegeAdmissionsWebcast.com.

CHAPTER 19

KILLER EXTRA CURRICULAR ACTIVITIES

How to Load Your Resume With Activities So Moving Your Admission Officer Will Choke Up, Lower Lip quivering Until She Breaks Into Uncontrollable Sobs, Crying "Someone - Anyone - HELP ME! We MUST Get This Kid On Our Campus!"

Let's take a look at some examples of compelling extra-curricular activities. But before I dive in, a comment.

I am not insisting that you come up with a bunch of stuff that "looks good" on the college application. You know what I mean, joining clubs just so you're "well-rounded" or running track if you hate to sweat.

In other words, don't do "stuff" just for college.

On the other hand, you should be willing to try things that are out of your comfort zone. Maybe you hate running, but want to challenge yourself by joining the cross country team, just to see you can do it. That's awesome!

On the other, other hand[18], it would be double-awesome to do something that:

1. Is related to something you love to do, or are at least strongly interested in; and

2. Most other teens would never do it

---

[18] That's three hands, if you're keeping score at home.

It's a cliche, but you will get average results in college admissions (or in life, Grasshopper) by doing the same things that everyone else does.

You'll get above average results if you are willing to do things that are different than what everyone else does.

Let's look at some activities that, although rewarding, are not going to make you stand out from the pack:

- Being a member of a club

- Being a member of a team

- Volunteering

- Most paid-for summer activities like teen tours, building houses somewhere in Latin America for a week, spending three days in the Israeli Army (I know your early morning hike up the mountain changed your life when you reached the top and surveyed below...)

I'm not calling into question the VALUE of these activities. I am pointing out that their impact for the narrow purposes of getting into college is limited, at best.

Actually, the paid-for summer activity can sometimes hurt you, because these kinds of things reek of privilege and can give off an unwanted message, "Mommy and Daddy can afford to send me on an 'enrichment' trip."

You should be interested to know that most college administrators, from presidents to admissions officers, hail from more modest, middle-class backgrounds and did not have similar enrichment opportunities. So bragging about this kind of life-changer may product an eye-roll, not necessarily a thick envelope stuffed with an offer of admission!

Here are some Atypical Teen Activities:

- Founding a club

- Captaining a team

- Being named All-Conference for a sport

- Interning or "Shadowing" an adult engaged in a profession you're considering

- Displaying your art in public

- Starting a business

- Self-publishing a book

- Publishing a blog

How many ATA's do you need?

Answer: not many. Maybe two or three, at most. In many cases, one is great.

Talk to any admissions officer, they'll tell you they are not impressed by an extracurricular list that goes on for pages, they'd rather see DEPTH, not breadth.

Final comment: I'm sick of hearing about how kids need to find their "passion."

The P Word has become so overused that it has lost meaning, but maybe I'm being a little too crabby (Moi?).

In my practice, I often hear from chagrined parents, who, with a shrug of their shoulders and an embarrassed, slight shake of the head, confide softly, Jordan just hasn't found his PASSION yet.

Look, I've found my passion and it isn't doing much for me. Do you know anyone who will pay me to sit on the couch and watch the Red Sox?

Passion is overrated. Seriously, how many 16 year old kids can identity their life calling?

My advice for these lazy, abhorrent, kids:

SEE A SPECIALIST! There's something wrong with you.

Seriously, pick something you're kind of interested in, that you can see yourself possibly getting into, and run with it. Give it a shot. It could develop into a strong interest, and possibly even a P Word.

Example:. Let's say you or your kid is interested in a career in marketing, so she ends up interning at an advertising or PR firm.

Your worst case scenario ain't bad: she sees what people do all day in this business, hates it, and avoids going down a long, painful - and expensive path!

I had a college friend whose father was an orthopedic surgeon, a Harvard guy.

My friend's grandfather was a pioneering, Harvard orthopedic surgeon.

My buddy didn't get into Harvard Med, but went another highly competitive medical school. He did his residency - in orthopedics - at a local hospital on Long Island.

He quit in less than three months.

What happened? I asked.

I just couldn't see myself doing this when I'm 40 or 50.

Dude, you serious? If anyone should have known what the life of an orthopod is like, it's a guy who's father and grandfather have that job!

He's what I call a "Smart Moron." Ultimately, he went back to school, got trained as a pathologist and has a great, 9-5 job. But he spent the extra money - and time - to get re-trained.

So the worst case scenario if you hate your internship is that you avoid this long, expensive, frustrating path.

Or maybe you end up loving what you see, and find out that people in that job aren't all geniuses, perhaps learning that they too are insecure and not always 100% certain about things. You build confidence.

But you're constructing a resume that not only looks good for colleges, but it's now starting to show that you possess skills that make you EMPLOYABLE!

And who knows, maybe you pick up a few contacts along the way, which could help your future networking efforts.

Chances are that you'll love interning. There's zero downside, the way I see it. Go for it!

CHAPTER 20

COLLEGE FINANCIAL PLANNING FOR THE 97% WHO DON'T HAVE ENOUGH SAVED FOR COLLEGE (OR HAVE IT BUT DON'T FEEL LIKE GETTING RIPPED OFF)

The College Board estimates that 97% of families don't have enough saved for college. Of course, they used to be in the student lending business before they executed a settlement (with the New York and Connecticut attorneys general) and hastily closed down operations...

...But I digress. let's assume that they're accurate. There are all sorts of crazy statistics about how much college costs have increased (more than 1,000% in the past 25 years, double the rate of inflation (300%), faster than every other benchmark like medical costs (700%), etc.)

What is the average family to do?

I wrote a book about this, *How to Pay "Wholesale" for College*, which I geared toward "Forgotten Middle Class" families - people who assume that they earn too much to qualify for anything.

Here's a smidge of advice from that Instant Classic (fairly described as a cross between *War and Peace* and *50 Shades of Gray*, but about financial aid):

First, many colleges will discount off their published "sticker" price. I'm referring mostly to private colleges, who have their own endowment resources to give out.

A survey of the National Association of College and University Business Officers revealed that the average discount rate for full-time freshmen enrolled at private colleges and universities was 52.4% in 2019. This percentage has increased six years in a row. (The average discount for all undergraduates - private and public - is 46%.)

That's why you should use a college's "sticker price" as a starting point only.

Who gets these discounts?

Perhaps not who you think. As far back as 2003, *The Nation* reported that 3% of of the students receiving financial aid at the top 146 colleges were from the bottom quartile of income earners.

A whopping 74% were from the top quartile, i.e. mostly six-figure-earning families.

Why are colleges discounting affluent families? To put butts in seats.

Their strategy is to offer $15,000 off to a family who can come up with the other $45,000. Over four years, that family is worth $180,000 plus to the college, not too shabby!

But colleges have competition - from each other. Out of the 2,800-odd four year schools, only about 90 admit 50% or less.

The vast majority of colleges are easy to get into!

And many of them compete with each other for a shrinking body of students.

The industry term is "pricing power," and it's weakening. *Inside Higher Ed* quoted an NACBO officer:

We are finding that our decision to increase tuition is less elastic than in previous years. More and more families are 'setting' the amount of tuition they are willing to pay, making it more difficult to increase net tuition revenue by increasing our sticker price.

In other words, the old "trick" of raising the published, or "sticker" price, then offering discounts, isn't working as well for non-elite private colleges (those that accept more than 50% of applicants) with more limited endowment funds.

Each college posts a "Net Price Calculator" on its website. Although they are flawed, using these calculators is a good way to see whether you could qualify for any discounts.

They're flawed because there is no standardized format used by all colleges, so some calculators ask for wages, some ask for your income plus retirement contributions (the latter is more accurate).

The other drawback is that the calculators do not suggest ways to improve eligibility. I already told you about *How to Pay "Wholesale" for College*, but there are other good resources on this topic too: Finaid.org and a great book called *How to Pay for College Without Going Broke* by Chany.

What a Financial Aid Office Examines

The most important set of financial information that a college financial aid office will look at comes from the calendar year that starts **two years before the year the student graduates from high school,** called the "Base Year."

You need to understand the financial aid formulas. (This is a simplified explanation, so don't get all annoying with me if you spot something that isn't 100% correct.)

Income is the most heavily weighted factor (you are penalized between 22-47% of your Adjusted Gross Income, meaning an extra $10,000 of income could reduce your eligibility for grants and loans by $2,200-$4,700 per year.

Assets are not penalized as severely: money in a parent's name is assessed 5.64%.

Money in a child's name, on the other hand, is penalized 20%-25%!

$100,000 in a parent's name reduces eligibility by $5,640 per year.

But the same $100,000 in a child's name could reduce eligibility by $20,000-25,000 per year!

Before you go pulling money out of child savings accounts willy-nilly[19], you need to explore the negative consequences (i.e. early withdrawal penalties) versus the potential benefits.

Let's look at the popular 529 account. Under the federal rules, the 529 is treated as a parent asset (which is good - it's penalized at the lower parental 5.64% instead of 20-25%).

However, I (and some of my colleagues across the country) are of the opinion that private colleges, using their own "Institutional Methodology" of calculating financial need, ignore the federal methodology and treat 529 accounts at a higher, child penalty rate of 20-25%.

So if you were reasonably certain that your child was likely to end up at a private college, AND you had substantial assets saved in a 529, your next move would be to figure out whether it pays to "shelter" the 529.

In other words, if you sell your 529 early, paying the penalty, would the subsequent eligibility improvement offset the negative aspects of this tactic?

If you sell a 529 before the calendar year in which you would incur "qualified" educational expenses (i.e. tuition, room and board) you are subject to a 10% penalty on the earnings in the 529 account.

So, assuming you have earnings (sadly, not always the case!) of $5,000 in your 529, you would pay a penalty of $500, but you could increase your eligibility by 20-25%.

The other cost associated with this transaction is that you may have to recapture any state tax deductions you may have taken when you

---

[19] Yes, I actually speak this way. Gotta problem, Daddy-O?

contributed to your 529 plan. This varies by state, so check this, and all of this advice, with your accountant.

Last comment, because this discussion is way outside the scope of this book: some assets don't count against you AT ALL. I'm referring to some annuity and insurance products and certain business assets. I cover this in *How to Pay "Wholesale" for College.* [20]

If you are interested in trying to improve your eligibility for need-based financial aid, your best bet is to look at these strategies before child's Junior year.

Put another way, if you're going to sell stuff off and create tax consequences, you'd better keep this paper trail off your tax return for your Base Year.

Final comment (really, this time I mean it) - this is GENERAL information, NOT specific advice about your unique situation. Talk with an accountant or other professional advisor about your specific situation.

RESOURCE: Learn how to "game" the system and obtain discounts of 45% or more, no matter how much you earn, at (c'mon, you can guess this one...) www.CollegeAdmissionsWebcast.com!

---

[20] Hmmm, another shameless plug.

CHAPTER 21

IF I TELL THEM I WANT FINANCIAL AID WILL IT HURT MY CHANCES OF GETTING IN?

Should I Check the "Yes" Box?

Will indicating that you want financial aid hurt your chances of admission?

Many parents and students believe that if they DO NOT check that box, they increase their chances of getting in, even if a college claims it does not care whether or not you want financial aid ("Need-Blind").

The rationale is that, because college is a business, they want a certain amount of kids paying full price - they'll admit them first, ahead of kids who cannot pay full fare.

In other words, if you can afford to pay the full cost of attendance, your chances of getting in are just a smidge better.

I won't lie[21], this is not an easy question to answer. Because there's no hard, statistical evidence one way or the other.

But understand the following points about this issue:

First, hardly any admissions officer in America will say - on the record - that full-pay students get priority consideration.

(This is not to say that they will get no consideration. Students with lower grades, but from affluent families likely to donate to the

---

[21] (To your face. :)

college, are considered "Development" cases. Most colleges allocate space in their incoming classes for these students.)

A few years ago, the New York Times published an article describing how Reed College's admissions office were asked to remove 100 qualified students in the "needs aid" pile and replace them with "full-pay" students.

Reed was not the only institution forced to make such decisions.

Thanks to lousy college endowment investment returns, many schools have changed their policies. My alma mater, Wesleyan University, is an example of a need-blind school that shifted its approach: in 2013, the president informed alumni that 90% of its next class would be admitted on a need-blind basis, while 10% would be "need-aware." In other words, for about 70 of its incoming class of 700 students, the admissions committee would consider whether the applicant needed financial aid in addition to the other criteria considered (grades, strength of curriculum, standardized test scores etc.).

I believe that many formerly need-blind schools will adopt this model, or that they're already doing behind closed doors.

The decision to apply for aid is important, but not nearly as meaningful as many parents think. Consider the situation at the most selective colleges.

Through establishing a superior brand and by aggressive marketing efforts, America's most prestigious colleges have created rabid demand for their spots.

The result is that the most competitive admit less than 15% of applicants.

And their wait lists regularly exceed one thousand applicants, each. They don't have an issue filling their slots because demand exceeds supply.

Financial Aid offices and admissions offices balance the amount of full-price-paying kids with those receiving tuition discounts.

It might be 75% who want aid, 25% who do not request it, for example.

But as long as the top colleges enjoy an oversupply of applicants for their slots, their admissions offices will have no problem filling their classes up with each type of student.

That's why I say that, if your student is qualified to get in, it's relatively immaterial whether he or she needs scholarships, grants or student loans. Sure, in some, rare cases, it can help marginally.

But let's say that you simply cannot float the cost without assistance from the college, but you do not check off the "Yes" box because you're a wee bit nervous, even though it may be irrational.[22]

Then your child gets in, and you quickly submit a financial aid application. Now what?

I can tell you from innumerable off-the-record, late night comments at boring conferences that admissions and financial aid officers "get" that you're trying to game the system. You're not fooling anybody.

Will they deny you every last cent of financial aid? Possibly.

Recently, two of my clients intentionally missed the priority deadline for financial aid in order to boost chances of admission, waited to get in, got admitted, then submitted their financial aid forms.

Each of the two colleges told them, Sorry, you're not eligible for anything - you missed the deadline.

Luckily, we were able to convince them to make an exception. We told each college that we did not bother applying because we figured

---

[22] I am not judging, I am superstitious too.

that we would not have qualified, which was stretching the truth, to say the least. (Don't judge me either!)

I recommend starting out on the right foot with your new relationship with the college. If you need financial aid, be upfront and honest about it.

If you get in, but can't afford to go, what good is your thick envelope?

But if you're willing to roll the dice, it's a different story. I had a client, Shannon, a widow, whose daughter was a top student and had dreamed of attending Brown University.

Shannon asked me in September of her daughter's Senior year, Will we improve her chances of getting in by not checking the financial aid box?

I asked her why Brown was her top choice.

Shannon replied that it "just was" and that, because she lost her husband in a tragic accident only three years earlier, Shannon wanted to support her daughter anyway she could. She felt that was what her late husband would have wanted, too.

So I told her NOT to check the box.

Why?

Mostly out of superstition, which I sheepishly confessed.

Even if there were a ½ of 1% chance that it could affect Shannon's daughter's application, I didn't want her to be denied, and then wonder about it for years.

What happened? She applied early, without submitting a financial aid application.

She was deferred to the "regular" pool (many competitive colleges do this instead of issuing an outright denial)...

...Two months later, she got in!

In April, we quickly submitted her financial aid application, although the deadline was November.

Brown responded in May, and the news wasn't great - they offered loans and work-study.

In other words, none of their own institutional endowment money.

Shannon understood that not applying for aid was a risk, and had the funds to put her daughter through college, thanks to life insurance proceeds. But she wasn't exactly happy.

We submitted an appeal, and waited. Two weeks went by.

Then, great news! Shannon received a thoughtful, personal letter from a financial aid officer, who increased her award from zero to more than $17,000 for that year!

Shannon and I were elated, because we had low expectations!

Somewhere up there, Shannon's husband was smiling too.

.

CHAPTER 22

OVERLOOKED DEADLINES

Don't get caught with your pants down!

There are two kinds of deadlines in the college planning process. Most families focus on only one: application deadlines. We'll look at those first.

Early Action, Early Decision and Regular Decision Deadlines

There are two types of college application deadlines: early and "regular."

"Early" means either "Early Decision" (binding on the applicant of admitted) or "Early Action" (non-binding). I discuss the implications of each later on.[23]

Most kids, parents and guidance counselors are familiar with deadlines for early applications (although last week I heard a disappointing story about a guidance counselor in an otherwise great district, giving his student incorrect advice that caused the student to miss one).

Many early deadlines are November 1, November 15, December 1. You need to check each college's website, because they vary. Do NOT rely on anyone else to give you this info, you must look it up yourself on each college's website.

---

[23] Ooooo. Cliffhanger.

Financial Aid Priority Deadlines

The second kind of deadline is the college's PRIORITY financial aid deadline, which, for many schools, coincides with the early application (for admission) deadlines.

NOTE - is not always easy, even for a seasoned (unindicted) college advisor like moi, to FIND these deadlines! Sometimes it takes 17 frustrating clicks to find the correct dates, required forms and other information you need. Gee, do you think that colleges really want you to find this stuff out?

The early financial aid deadline is designed so that the school can give you a preliminary financial aid award by December, right after it admits you Early Decision.

Note: the only "out" for Early Decision applicants relates to financial considerations. If you get in ED, but cannot afford to attend the college, you may ask the college to release you from your obligation and withdraw your application for admission.

If you are applying regular decision, same deal - make sure you research the school's priority financial aid deadlines. In many cases, financial aid awards are given first-come, first served.

Here's a tip: Pearl (who files 400+ financial aid applications each year) will submit ALL financial aid apps before the earliest deadline, this way she doesn't have to worry about missing later deadlines at other colleges.

Note: if you batch out your first set of financial aid apps, then later decide to apply for ADMISSION to a few more colleges[24], **you must also submit your FAFSA, etc. to those new schools too.** There is no automatic updating, you must file manually.

---

[24] Perhaps because your kid spazzes out and panics, thinking he'll never get in anywhere.

The FAFSA allows you to electronically port over income information from your tax returns using the IRS Data Retrieval Tool. This usually works, but there have been glitches in the past. So try it, unless your you file your taxes by mail, instead of electronically.

Other colleges that require the CSS Profile financial aid form want you to transmit copies of your returns using a service called IDOCS. Still others want IRS Tax Transcripts. They will tell you their requirements.

So if you "low-balled" your estimated income and received a conditional award based on those figures, you should know that your award, and everything you indicate on your financial aid application, is subject to review and adjustment.

I realize that I just packed in a lot of information in these paragraphs. If you want more info, come join the fun online on our webinar, www.FinancialAidWebcast.com.

In summary: remember that your admissions application deadline is only part of the picture. **Research the priority financial deadlines for each and every college on your list.**

CHAPTER 23

HOW TO WRITE AN ESSAY THAT DOESN'T SUCK

Also, what Stormy, The Kardashians and a decapitated body can learn ya, why your English teacher may be the worst source of advice...and the deadliest sin committed by college essay-writers

Most college essays suck. Really, really suck.

Why?

Before I get to that, let me give you a little "back story."

First, the college essay just isn't THAT important!

Shocked? Don't get your undergarments in a bunch.

The essay, or personal statement, is somewhat important, because it gives the reader of your application an opportunity to get to know more about you, beyond the transcripts and standardized test scores comprising your application.

It give you a chance to stand out.

But how important IS it?

My best guess is that the essay constitutes 10% of the application. 15% tops.

But if your credentials make you a 50-50% shot, meaning you have the "chops" on paper to get in but 7,000 other kids have the same academic credentials, that's where this 10% takes on greater import.

To understand how to write an "Essay So Compelling That Admissions Officers Will Crawl Naked Over Broken Glass To Admit Your Student," you should understand your reader.

Typically, an admissions officer has a stack of about four million applications to read by the end of the weekend. Yours is buried in that stack.

If your essay talks about "The plethora and myriad of leadership experiences" you aggregated during your four hours at the soup kitchen last Thanksgiving, you will lose her. Fast.

Another thought: you can get an "A" on your English paper by writing a left-brained essay: solid opening, well-developed body, strong conclusion, correct grammar and spelling.

But while your English paper gets you a great grade, there's one big reason why it could be a LOUSY college application essay:

It's B-O-R-I-N-G!

Your essay needs to cut through the clutter. A great essay will jump off the page, grab the overburdened, bored-out-of-her-skull reader by the throat, get eight centimeters from her face and scream in a shrill, spittle-spraying voice, "READ ME, DAMNIT! THIS IS WHO I AM! YOU'D BE A MORON NOT TO ADMIT ME!!!!"

(Note to dumb readers: I don't mean literally.)

How do you stop her dead in her tracks? How do you learn this style of writing?

Here's an unconventional idea. Warning - if you mention you're doing this to a teacher or other "schmexpert" who knows everything, you will be ridiculed. Here's the tip:

Read the tabloids!

Example:

Headless Body In Topless Bar

That's the most famous headline ever to appear in the New York Post. Grabs your attention, doesn't it?

Sure, that's not exactly how your personal statement should start, but...

~Dead Horse Beater Alert~

You're recall that this process is not a meritocracy, it's about is marketing yourself? (I may have mentioned this once or 25 times.)

Great marketing gets a product - and a college applicant - noticed.

Your essay better do this, or your candidacy could die a sad, lonely death.

There's a reason why some of the highest paid writers on the planet create headlines for tabloids like the Enquirer and publications of that ilk - their job is to grab your attention.

Their task isn't easy, we are bombarded by 4,000 or more messages per day. So by the time we're at the checkout line at the supermarket, we're pretty numb, fried without realizing it.

So THAT'S why the latest gossip about the Kardashians[25] never fails to catch my eye!

And you? (If you claim you don't notice these things, you're either a dirty, rotten liar or a robot.)

So think of your essay like a modified tabloid, but keep the alien invasion theories to yourself.

Think of the first line of your essay as the headline, that telegraphs to the reader why she should read the second sentence.

The purpose of the second sentence? To get you to read the third. And so on.

---

[25] Especially if accompanied by prurient photographs.

Here's one of my all-time favorite essay openers from four or five years ago. It was written by a Jewish kid who attended a local parochial school - funny/interesting all by itself!

He told a nice story about how he overcame anti-Semitism and bullying initially to become president of this club, captain of that team, etc.

But he would not have earned the RIGHT to tell his story without a snappy, opening sentence that drew the reader in, promising a reward for continuing to read. His opener went something like this:

"So there I was, three years after my bar mitzvah, about to receive Communion, and…"

I'm smiling as I write this! How can you NOT want to read the rest?

Think "tabloid" when you write your college essay!

CHAPTER 24

SHOULD YOU TAKE 18 AP CLASSES?

What the hell else do you have to do all day, anyway?

Quick: what looks better to an admissions officer - a "C" in an AP course or an "A" in a regular class?

An "A" in the AP class! :)[26]

The real issue discussed in this chapter is whether a child should load up with every available AP in an effort to impress top colleges, so she gets in and earns a ton of merit scholarships.

The answer: "No."

Well, almost always "No."

The most important factor weighed by admissions committees is whether the student demonstrated mastery of tough, college-level material. In other words, did the student take challenging classes and earn high marks?

Is the student interested in challenging herself academically? Or did she "play it safe," going for a high GPA at the expense of learning ("grade grubbing").

Top colleges like to see applicants who showed a thirst for learning, for pushing themselves and achieving. If an applicant had an opportunity to take a tough course, but chose not to, an admissions officer will take note.

---

[26] You were hoping for advice like this when you bought this book. You're welcome (go leave that 5 star review).

So my hard-ass advice is[27], if you want to get into an ultra-competitive college, push yourself.

Even if you're not striving for a super-elite school, I would err on the side of taking on too much. It's easier to drop down from an advanced class, much harder to do the opposite.

What courses count the most? "Core" classes: English, math, science, language and history for liberal arts schools. Of course music and art classes count for specialty colleges and programs in those areas.

By the way, AP and IB courses are treated the same by practically all admissions officers. But AP and Honors are not. Here's why:

AP is deemed more rigorous because it represents materials that adhere to a nationally recognized curriculum. In theory, AP US History should cover the same material in New York as the same class in Portland, Oregon and Portland, Maine.

In contrast, a local school can decide what constitutes an "Honors" class. An Honors English class in Chevy Chase, Maryland can in theory be entirely unrelated to Honors English in Bloomfield Hills, Michigan.

So, yes, AP and IB classes signal that you have challenged yourself. But hear me now and believe me later - taking challenging courses is great, but only if you're going to pull an A or a B.

NOT a C.

A common scenario in my practice is when a child, who excels in one area such as English, History or writing, feels pressure to take AP Physics because it will "look good" on her college applications.

However, she has less than zero interest in majoring in science in college. And she feels like she'd be lucky to pull a C in the class.

---

[27] Which I freely admit that I would have blown off when I was in high school...

I realize that you cannot predict the future, but you should be able to make an educated projection.

Yes, it's true that admissions officers look at weighted and unweighted grades. Maybe an AP C equals a non-AP B in abstract terms.

But psychologically, a C stands out more in a transcript compared to a B, even though it may have resulted from a less challenging class.

If the student blows off AP Physics, does it mean that she'll never get into Princeton?

Put it this way, it won't help her cause, because it will demonstrate that she could not excel in a college level class. And bear in mind that she could be competing with other applicants who took 18 APs.

The bigger question posed by the "Should I take AP Physics" issue is whether she wants to go to a school like Princeton.

If the answer is "No," I'll advise 100 out of 100 kids like her not to kill themselves with AP Physics.

But if the answer is "Yes," or "Maybe," then get out the Adderall (prescribed, not black market), 4 Hour Energy pills and whatever else you need to help you with the required workload.

But in all seriousness, please, be careful. It's one thing to push yourself, it's another to put your health in jeopardy. And I was half-joking about the pills. I'm no doctor. See the movie *Race to Nowhere* for some sobering insight.

What if I challenge myself and still get a bad grade?

Most admissions officers at competitive schools will reassure you not to be freaked out by one isolated bad grade.

As a matter of fact, they like kids who overcome challenges. So do ALL of us "regular" folks.

167

The story of a hero who failed, but doubled his effort, found a mentor and fought back to succeed, is an archetypal story line that goes back 4,000 plus years to ancient Greece, probably even further!

All humans respond to this type of story, that's why formulaic movies like Rocky draw millions of fans, no matter how predictable.

So if you bomb a class, chill out, put it behind you and work harder! Go on your own "Hero's Journey!"

CHAPTER 25

ARE YOU "INTERESTED?"

How to weasel your way into college by Haskell-style, strategic brown-nosing

Are you interested?

Loaded question, I know. Let me explain why you need to understand this concept in order to stack the admissions odds in your favor.

Demonstrating interest is the ONE factor that is easily and completely in your control, unlike grades, standardized test scores, recommendations and other stuff subject to the moods and whims of third parties.

About three years ago, I was chatting on the phone with a client who told me about her friend, Molly. Molly's daughter was rejected from the University of Delaware, while her friend's kid, with lower grades and scores was admitted.

So Molly did what any card-carrying Helicopter Parent would do: called the admissions office and demanded an explanation!

Instead of telling her to go commit an unnatural act, as I might have done, the admissions officer very professionally agreed to pull up Molly's daughter's file.

"I see here that Molly never visited campus and took a tour. We didn't think she was interested in coming here," the admissions officer told her.

"I can't go into details, but your daughter's friend did that and much more, which indicated that she was seriously considering us," she said.

169

She was talking about "Expressed Interest."

In a nutshell, students who show more interest in a college have greater chances of getting in! Because admissions officers are watching like "Big Brother."

I'm not exaggerating, many colleges use software that tracks and "scores" each candidate's activities that demonstrate interest. Big Data has come to college admissions.

> Tip: The website CollegeData.com publishes what colleges self-report about how much they consider interest, as well as a lot of other valuable information.

I can sense you rolling your eyes, but let me explain how you can play the game to win...

...And why this matters so much to each college. (Don't shoot the messenger! FYI, I think it's a little creepy, but it ain't changing as far as I can see, so deal with it...)

First, let me give you some examples of how you can show interest. I recommend doing as many of the following as you can.

- Sending away for written information via response card in EVERY piece of mail the college sends you

- Filling out an online form at the college's website

- Having your guidance counselor contact the college on your behalf

- Introducing yourself to a representative at a college night

- Chatting online with that rep or another

- Calling the school to ask questions/set up an interview

- Visiting the college, taking a tour

- Speaking to the department heads in the areas of study you're considering

- Interviewing with the admissions office

- Interviewing with a local alum

- Sending a handwritten thank you note to each person you met

- Logging into the college's portal for prospective students (they check, if you have never logged in, they will think you are not interested!)

- Writing a check for $6M[28]

Now, it's important NOT to cross a line and become a stalker.

Creepiness rarely helps your chances of getting admitted....

So don't call the admissions office hourly, daily or too frequently.

How frequent is too frequent? My rule of thumb is that you should not call unless you have something relatively important or interesting to ask or say.

Once a month sounds like a lot, but if you think long and hard about it, I'm sure you can come up with significant, interesting questions or other tidbits more or less on this schedule.

Why is expressing interest so important?

It's all about rankings. Here's how it works.

- More interest from you translates into a higher likelihood that you'll go to that college if they admit you.

---

[28] Nothing like making the same joke, over and over.

- This helps the college's "Yield," the golden ratio and a critical rankings factor considered by US News and World Report. Yield is calculated by dividing the number of students admitted by the number of kids who enroll. The higher the yield, the more attractive the college looks, the higher the rankings.

- The higher the yield, the better the school's bond ratings. So when it goes to borrow for those new dorms or $100 Million athletic complex, their interest rate will be lower that a college with a lower yield.

That's more than enough information than you need. You get the point - show them that you're interested!

Chapter 26

Beyond The Tour

"Wicked Smaht" Questions To ask

It's no secret - all college brochures, websites and other marketing materials look pretty much the same: a smiling selection of acne-free, multi-ethnic, thin students frolicking on the quad (even if the school is in Minnesota, where it's warm three days per academic year).

How do you get the truth about what it's like to attend a particular school?

Guidebooks and websites (I like Fisk's and CollegeConfidential.com) are a good place to start, but bear in mind that each commentator has his own axe to grind. Just because one kid complained about access to professors, or excessive drinking, you name it, does not mean that you would have an identical experience if you attended that school.

Ditto for advice from your cousin, or the neighbor's older daughter - they may love or hate a certain school, but, chances are, you are not 100% aligned with their opinions about everything.

My advice is to start with the above, then drill down.

There's no substitute for a campus visit, if you can find the time to go while school is in session. Here are a few (OK, 14) thoughts:

1. Let the student - not mom or dad - do most of the questioning of a tour guide.

2. If you hate the tour guide, or presentation by someone in admissions, bear in mind that each has little to do with students' experiences at that college.

3. Ditto if you love the tour guide or presentation.

4. Grab a campus newspaper - see what's being talked about, both negative and positive. This may be the best way to get insight on the main issues students are talking about.

5. Go to the career center. Ask about internships and other support services they offer. Find out which employers recruit on campus. Ask about the alumni network - how supportive is it, what makes it different than other colleges. Ask what they would advise any incoming freshmen.

6. Eat the food in the student center or dining hall. (You could be there four years, you'll eat a lot over that period!)

7. Chill out - without parents around - in the student center or other place where kids congregate. Tell your parents to take a walk for 45 minutes or so. Keep your ears and eyes wide open, soak in the experience. Ask yourself, "Can I see myself here, with these kids, for four years?"

8. Talk to students, ask them what they like about the school, what they dislike, what other schools did they consider and how did they end up choosing this one.

9. Attend a class (arrange this with admissions ahead of time).

10. Talk to a department head or a professor in a field you're considering. Tell him/her you're considering majoring in that field, ask what advice they would give. Mention other colleges you're considering, ask how their school differs.

11. If you'll require support (example, for learning disabilities), sit down with the appropriate support program head. Ask how one goes about obtaining support, are there extra fees, how does their program differ from other colleges.

12. If you're an athlete, meet with a coach (usually an assistant but frequently the head coach is available). Talk to kids currently on the team. If you can connect with parents of

athletes, get their perspective on what it's like to play for that school, especially the coach's style, their academic support services for athletes. Try to speak to recently graduated students (get their contact info from the coach) about their experiences, what they'd do if they had to do it all over again, etc.

13. If you're a performing artist, do the equivalent of the things I recommend for student-athletes.

14. Take notes, immediately! School visits tend to blend together, so I urge you to jot down your thoughts during and immediately after you visit. It doesn't matter whether you hand write or thumb type your notes, just get 'em down, keep 'em organized for future reference.

RESOURCE: Go to www.CollegeAdmissionsWebcast.com for more questions to help evaluate whether a college is a good fit

CHAPTER 27

HOW NOT TO SCREW UP YOUR INTERVIEW

We have already discussed[29] the idea of demonstrating Interest via a variety of activities. Interviewing is one of the big ones.

Yet, while nerve wracking to most students, interviews are just not THAT important. Many colleges do not require them, as a matter of fact. So do not get too hyper if you have one scheduled. (Feel better?)

True, interviews (either the local alum at Starbucks/Panera variety or the "official," on campus kind) let the college know that you are seriously considering it, and they allow the interviewer to get a glimpse of your personality...especially the side that's nervous when meeting authority figures in artificially stressful environments. :)

You may be surprised, perhaps comforted, to know that a major purpose of the interview has nothing to do with you, actually. Colleges use alumni interviews as a tool to make the alum feel connected to the school, not because you're a shoe-in there.

So don't read too much into it if you hear that a local Harvard or Princeton alum wants to chat.

My best advice is to try to have fun. I know that "fun" is probably not the word that springs to mind when you think about interviewing, but it could. Here's what I mean.

Think of the interview of your opportunity to ask the representative from the college questions you want answered.

---

[29] "Discussed" isn't really the right word, this is more like a giant filabuster.

In other words, YOU are interviewing them.

Easier said than done? Maybe.

But remember, colleges are businesses. They compete with other colleges for paying customers - you. So why not turn the tables on them?

If you're nervous about your first interview, it's OK. You should be, you've never done this before.

Consider scheduling a "dry run" interview at a local college, one that you have no strong intention of attending. This makes things a lot less stressful when you have your next, "real" interview.

(It also makes you feel good to tease a poor, hapless interviewer who undoubtedly will covet your attention, attracted by objects she cannot have. That was a joke. Sorta.)

I think the main reason kids get nervous about interviews is because they are afraid of the unknown. So this "fake" interview lets you get a practice one under your belt, turning the unknown into the routine.

Speaking of "belt," let me offer a few grooming tips. (Ironically, I would not want you to see me writing this, as it's 5:45 am, I'm in my ratty gym clothes).

I'm making these comments only because I've had more than one last-minute, we're-driving-to-the-interview, "emergency" phone calls from parents along the lines of, "Can you please tell Brandon he should shave?" Or, "Tell Jared that he can't wear shorts!"

Sigh...

Here's my advice about what to wear. Think "country club casual." I'm not exactly sure what that means, but I know that Pearl tells me all the time that I'm not allowed to wear jeans on the rare occasion that I'm invited to a club for dinner.

So khakis and a golf shirt, or the equivalent, are fine if you're a guy. I'm not sure what that translates into for a girl. A sun dress? Refer to your nearest J Crew catalog.

You don't need to wear a suit or formal dress, either.

You should "mirror" - or dress slightly nicer than your interviewer, who is not likely to be in a stuffy coat and tie. He's more likely to be in a button down shirt and khakis, but not jeans.

And yes, hair should be brushed, teeth brushed, guys should shave. It shows that you respect your interviewer and the process.

Interview Questions to Prepare For

In every interview, be ready to answer questions about yourself and why you are interested in that college. Examples:

- Tell me about yourself (technically, not a question but be prepared to respond!)
- What is your favorite class?
- Who is your favorite teacher?
- Does your high school record accurately reflect your ability?
- What is the last book you read for pleasure?
- What do you do with your free time?
- What made you consider [College]?
- What questions do you have for me about [College]?
- Tell me about a challenge you overcame.

Instead of providing you a script to memorize, let's discuss some common denominator, thematic responses.

Prepare. There really are no "wrong" answers to any of these, or other questions...

Except any answer that shows a lack of thought will make you look dumb, immature and ill-prepared. Which is not the end of the world, for the most part, since the interview is relatively unimportant. But if you can nail the interview, you'll only help your cause.

As I was working on this section, a client reminded me how her daughter answered the interview question, "Why are you interested in Babson?"

Her reply: "Um, you have a pretty campus!"

She still got in.

Please prepare a little more than my client. Research things the college says about itself online and the major you're considering. What special programs or courses do they feature? What is the background (publications, career experience) of the department heads and professors? Look through the course catalog, each college publishes it online.

Another comment on the "Why are you considering X College?" question: do not cite generic, non-school-specific answers, such as "I've always wanted to go to school in Boston, Washington D.C., etc." There are scores of colleges in your desired area, so that answer shows a lack of thought.

Your answers should demonstrate that you're a reasonably smart, thoughtful, friendly and enthusiastic applicant. Not a whiny, boring complainer - no-one likes negativity. (Admissions officers never say, "Hey, enough Intel finalists and team captains, already, get me a negative, entitled kid, wouldya?")

Here are some technical tips.

- Look at the interviewer in the eye when you meet. Give a firm, dry handshake.

- Smile often and easily - we're talking about a kind, pleasant smile - not a manic, rabid-dog-like fang display or twisted grimace.

- Maintain eye contact - do not look downward at your crotch or smartphone. But don't stare in a creepy, unblinking crazy-eyed way.

- Do not blab. Answer the question asked, expand to show that you're thoughtful, but do not go off on a 90 minute diatribe.

- Remember that your interviewer is a person, too. Don't be afraid to ask him/her questions about their experience at that college (assuming they attended that school), which other colleges they considered when they were applying, and how they feel that this college is different from other competitor colleges.

(Incidentally, I love that last question - it shifts the power in the interview, not the interviewer is "selling" the college to you!)

Do not answer calls that come to your cell phone during your interview. (Real story.)

If you mistakenly answer a call mid-interview, do not chit chat for a minute or three before hanging up. (Real story.)

Do not take your parents with you on your interview. (Sadly, many real stories.)

As you can deduce from these examples of what NOT to do, there is a really, really low standard out there for teens' behavior.

But that's great news for you! All you need to do to distinguish yourself is simple stuff, like show that you have half a brain and are somewhat prepared, make eye contact and keep your damn phone locked away somewhere.

Note to the introverted, quiet or shy: you are normal. Do not join Toastmasters or Dale Carnegie for college interview purposes only. Just be yourself, but a slightly more outgoing version of yourself that wants to create a good first impression. You do not have to act like a used car salesman.

Ask someone whom you respect, but aren't necessarily best friends with, to "mock" interview you.

Who? Like your school principal. Or teacher.

Another idea: video yourself answering the basic questions listed in this chapter. Then watch, critically, asking yourself:

Did I make eye contact?

Was I fidgety?

Did I mumble?

Summary - the interview is not that important, but every little bit helps. Relax, prepare, try to enjoy the process. Since that's probably impossible, fake your enjoyment - give 'em a smile and you'll probably convince your interviewer and yourself that you're having a good time.

CHAPTER 28

RECOMMENDATION
RECOMMENDATIONS

What teachers to ask, when to ask, how to procure a glowing letter even if your teacher wouldn't know you if he ran over you in the parking lot, how many is "too many?

Most colleges request two teacher recommendations and a write-up from your guidance counselor. Whom do you ask?

My preference is for kids to ask teachers of academic classes (not Phys Ed., generally). It's nice to show one "left-brained" subject, i.e. math or science and one "right-brained" class such as English or History, but certainly not necessary, so don't sweat it if you cannot.

However, if you are applying to college pre-med, and the only subjects represented by recommendations are US History and English, you could raise an eyebrow on the admission committee. The absence of a Biology or Chemistry teacher raises a red flag.

It's not enough for a teacher to say in a recommendation letter that you earned good grades. Selective colleges are looking to fill their classrooms with active, engaged, curious learners who participate. These traits deserve mention in a recommendation letter.

If that's not you, fine. If you were a quiet, "back of the classroom" type who didn't speak up too much, but did well academically, no harm in "coaching" your teacher by reminding him of your achievements. "Mr. Johnson, I really enjoyed your class and was hoping that you'd write my college recommendation for me. You may recall that I [blah blah blah]."

Incidentally, if you have any doubt about whether your teacher will write a good letter, the time to find out is before he puts pen to paper! There's nothing wrong with asking, Do you think you'd be able to write me a strong recommendation?

If you get an answer like "I'm not sure" or anything other than "yes," politely thank him and withdraw your request. Move on.

Another "teacher coaching" point: if you're asking an English teacher because you are considering a career in journalism, specifically state that to your teacher. It could help him focus his comments.

How many is too many? The temptation of excessive recommendations ("Thick File, Thin Applicant.")

Let me tell you how I ate crow last year. I have a client, Steve (not his real name), who's a real Alpha Male, Type A, entrepreneurial guy. He's very successful.

His daughter, Kelly (her real name. Just kidding, not her real name either), was a great kid and an above average student. Not a top scholar, but a serious, hard working kid.

Kelly wanted to go to a well-known, private school with much higher average SATs and GPAs than what she presented.

So Steve asked me, I'm friends with So and So, who's a big booster of the football team. Should I have him write a letter?

My answer: Do NOT go overboard. It's one thing to send a supplemental recommendation or two (Kelly's boss at the shelter she volunteered at sent a nice letter) from someone who knows the student in a non-academic capacity, it's another to load up her file with letters from strangers.

One of my favorite sayings is "Thick file,, THICK applicant," meaning, if a candidate's file is overloaded with letters from Senators, Supreme Court justices and other muckety-mucks, admissions officers generally roll their eyes and dismiss these endorsements as indications that Daddy or Mommy has connections that they are trying to use to get a mediocre kid into a college they otherwise could not get into.

So about six weeks after I told Steve Don't do it!, he left a five-minute, taunting message on my cell phone.

"Hah, Lockwood! She got in! Whoooo, yeah! Suck it! Don't ever doubt me again, baby!!!" (etc. etc. etc.)

Steve was gloating because he ignored my advice...and it paid off!

(I was slightly concerned that Kelly wouldn't be able to keep up with the workload at this school, so I had a talk with her. I told her that was entering another league and that I expected that she would rise to the occasion. Six months later, I ran into her when she was home on break. Kelly told me that was doing OK, dropped one course, was working her butt off, but getting mostly B's, which is great!)

Turns out, the excessive recommendations didn't hurt Kelly's chances. Let's look at the real reason she got in.

CHAPTER 29

UNPUBLISHED ADMISSIONS STATISTICS

There's never ONE REASON why a candidate is admitted to a college, although tempting to figure out. In the previously described case, one of the real reasons Kelly got into a school where her credentials were substantially below average: she was a "Development" case - admissions industry parlance for an affluent family who could become a donor to the university.

That's why for many competitive colleges, about two-thirds of the class is filled for non-academic reasons, according to *Admissions Confidential*, by Rachel Toor, former admissions officer at Duke University. Meaning that 66% or more of the class is comprised of developmental cases, athletes, musicians, minorities, international students, legacies and other special cases.

A smaller percentage, as low as 25% at some colleges, are admitted purely for academic reasons.

So if the published admissions rate is 15%, but you do not fall into a special category, your real odds might be 7% or less!

I tell kids with stellar achievements in high school and aspirations of elite colleges that, if they don't get in, it's not a question of whether they can do the work at those institutions.

I recall a quote from someone at Harvard along the lines of, "We could fill the class three times over with qualified applicants."

What do you do if you're a Plain White Kid or other "non-special" category?

(I'm sorry if I offended any white folk. My mother was white, and many of my friends are of the Caucasian Persuasion.)

Answer: you've got to stand out as an interesting kid, an Atypical Teen.

The other takeaway here is that, if you're in the middle of the college's reported GPA/SAT range, you should not become complacent and assume that you have a god shot at admission. Because that range includes the special category kids who tend to drag down those averages.

Final comment: Development List kids are not merely rubber stamped "Admitted" merely because their families donate a few million, even pre-Felicity. I've heard numerous stories of admissions officers denying Development List kids for a variety of reasons, including subpar academics, and coming off as entitled or arrogant.

I guess I should make one more note on development to round out the discussion: according to the National Association of Collegiate Business Officers, approximately 50 cents on the dollar goes to financial aid for low income families.

CHAPTER 30

EARLY DECISION: BAD DECISION?

How the Early Bird can get hosed, and who is ED designed to help, really?

I was reviewing Early Decision admissions stats a few years ago and found it tough to discern a trend. Some Ivies continue to see small increases in Early Decision applications (Brown, Dartmouth reported higher Early Decision numbers), while others showed decreases (Columbia, Cornell, Penn reported slightly lower numbers).

Overall admissions rates were slightly down across the board at the Ivies compared to the previous year:

- Harvard: 5.79%

- Yale: 6.72%

- Columbia: 6.89%

- Princeton: 7.29%

- Brown: 9.116%

- Dartmouth: 10.05%

- Penn: 12.10%

- Cornell: 15.15%

Rates for applicants applying ED are were higher across the board. (I could republish those percentages here but I don't feel like it. You get the point.) For some schools, you apparently double or triple your chances.

In other words, if the "raw," overall admissions rate is 10%, the ED rate could be 30%.

ED Helps Colleges, Not Kids

Let's look at two, oft-ignored points about ED. First, it was designed to help colleges, not students. How?

Competitive college fill about 40% of their class with ED applicants. Put another way, by December 15th, many colleges have almost half of their class filled. It takes the pressure off them to put "butts in seats," and allows them to relax after the New Year. Kind of like "Senior Slump" for admissions officers!

ED Can Hurt Your Wallet

Now let's explore the financial aid impact of ED. Most colleges will tell you that whether you apply ED has nothing to do with your financial aid package.

In other words, each applicant will receive a full and fair financial aid offer, without regard to whether he applied Early Decision or regular decision.

My opinion?

Dog poop.

Notwithstanding their reassurances, colleges don't always give their "highest and best" financial aid offer. If they did, they'd never revise their offers.

Every year, I sort through dozens of "lowball" financial aid offers that somehow magically improve after we appeal and negotiate them. (Covered briefly How to Pay "Wholesale" for College, more extensively in my online, on demand training, www.AppealsClass.com).

Another comment: there's an element of self-selection contained in the statistics, meaning stronger students, athletes, legacies, and other recruited "Hooks" apply ED.

Keep that in the back of your mind next time you're thinking about applying early.

Final thought: it's worth thinking about WHY a certain college emerges as the top choice for any given student.

Many times, it's an emotional reason (It just "felt right" from the moment I stepped on campus), which is fine, but it doesn't mean that you'll be miserable everywhere else if you don't get in.

All sorts of famous, successful people didn't get into their first choice school, such as Warren Buffett, but things turned out well despite the initial rejection.

It is perfectly OK to have five first choice schools. Especially when you step back and consider that, at each college, you'll pretty much be surrounded by the same types of upper-middle class kids, and your classes will be taught by similar professors, covering substantially the same subject matter. (Seriously, how different is Freshman English at Harvard compared to Vanderbilt, University of Delaware, University of Illinois or any other college?)

You may disagree, but deep down you know I'm right! (My theory: if I say I'm right, that means that I am, in fact, right.)

Resource: www.AppealsClass.com shows you all of the arguments you can possibly make to improve your financial aid offer after it's been given. In this on-demand training webinar, I cover how I increased a "final offer" of zero from Yale to $40,000 - per year, how we improved an offer from University of Southern California by more than $30,000 and other real life, proven examples.

CHAPTER 31

HOW TO IMPROVE A CRAPPY "FINAL" FINANCIAL AID AWARD AFTER IT'S BEEN ISSUED...

....Even if you don't have compromising pictures of the dean

In my workshops, I usually discuss how to appeal a "lowball" financial aid offer. Increases of $2,000, $5,000 and $10,000 per year are common, but of course not a sure thing.

This past year, two of my clients each received increases of more than $30,000. For one year.

Yesterday, a third client showed me the results of our appeal that changed her initial award of $3,000 to $31,500 in grants.

The most frequent common denominator in a successful appeal: applying strategically - to colleges that historically compete with one another - and playing them off against each other. Let's look at Rick's story.

When Rick and his daughter, Alexis, came to me, Alexis was a Junior.

She had identified USC. as her top choice college, and Rick wanted advice on how to afford a $58,000 per year (then) school.

After advising him on re-allocating his assets to improve his eligibility, I commented, "You'd be smart to apply to one or two "competitor-schools" to use as leverage.

Alexis said, "What do you mean, Pomona, UCLA, those types of schools?"

Yes, I said, but you should also look at Syracuse and George Washington, because Alexis was going to major in communications. I suggested these colleges even though it was on the opposite coast, and no parent would think of it as competing with USC.

Fast forward to March in Alexis' senior year. She gets into her dream school! She's psyched!

A week later, her financial aid award arrives. Rick is NOT psyched.

Even though USC offered a decent amount - $23,518 per year is a nice chunk of change (never a round number!) Rick needed a whole lot more to cover his costs.

Then the GW offer came: $40,000.

GW looked at the same financial aid forms (the CSS Profile and FAFSA) as USC, but came up with a much different award.

"What do I do? My friends are telling me that I'm nuts, I should take the 40K and send Alexis to GW. They say I'll never get another penny from USC," Rick said on the phone.

"Let's try to appeal the USC offer - maybe they'll come up a little," I responded.

Then we drafted an appeal letter, sent it, and waited. And waited.

Three weeks later, I received a voicemail, sent at 1:00 am, "Andy, you've got to help me, we haven't heard anything. Alexis is in her room, crying!"

I called Rick the next day. "They really should have gotten back to you by now. Do you have the original checklist I sent you with the draft of the appeal letter?" I asked.

Rick found my email, and we went through it together.

"Did you send it by email and regular mail?"

"Yes."

"Did you follow up the next day, to make sure they received it?"

"Yes."

"Did you send a copy to admissions?"

"Um..."

Rick forgot to cc the admissions officer in charge of Long Island. This turned out to be a fatal mistake.

Why was this important?

Admissions officers care about rankings. A key component of ranking is "Yield" - the ratio of admitted students versus matriculated students.

A higher yield means that the school is desirable, a lower yield means that too many students said, Thanks, but no thanks.

A strong yield indirectly equates not only to higher rank, but also to a stronger credit rating, which comes in handy the next time the college needs to borrow to build the next dorm, food court or other amenity - hey, climbing walls and lazy rivers don't come cheap!.

Generally, financial aid officers are "bean counters" and are not directly affected by yield and enrollment targets.

Rick slammed down the phone and immediately sent the appeal letter to Admissions.

Within hours, they called him.

"Did you send this letter to Chuc" in Financial Aid?" his officer asked.

"No, I've been dealing with someone else," Rick said.

"I'm going to walk down there and put this on his desk," his admissions officer said.

Rick told me that, within hours, Chuck - the "right guy" - called him, asked him a few questions about his business (Rick owns a restaurant) - and told him he'd reassess his award.

The revised offer came the next day: $53,540!

Rick was dumbfounded. His friends were shocked!

I was pretty surprised, too - I figured that USC would come up with another $10,000 or so.

Most importantly, Alexis was overjoyed - now she could go to her dream college!

What colleges compete with one another?

When I walk through "before and after" examples at presentations, I frequently get the question, How do you know which schools compete with each other?

Part of the answer is commonsensical - rival colleges in the same athletic conference, for example.

Cornell University is the only college I know that has stated, in writing, that they will consider this strategy! I tip my cap to them, because I appreciate their candor.

Other grounds for appealing a financial aid award

We can use the Cornell guidelines as a roadmap for appeals to all colleges. On their Financial Aid Appeal Application, Cornell cites the following categories of appeals they will consider:

    1. Significant loss of income due to termination or change of employment

    2. Unexpected life event ("Life Event" is one of my favorite financial aid terms - a neat, tidy way to summarize intense, emotionally trying situations like a divorce or other traumatic experience!)

    3. Correction to income or asset information reported

    4. More favorable award from another financial institution. Cornell then explains:

Cornell will review financial aid offers from any of the Ivy League institutions, Stanford University, Duke University, and MIT. NOTE: Early Decision Freshman cannot appeal for this reason.

Shazam! Cornell lays it all out, even identifying the other colleges they consider "rivals." Personally, I would have added a few schools to their list of rivals, namely Amherst College, Williams College and a handful of others.

But I appreciate how Cornell takes us appeal-minded folks behind the curtain and reveals all their secrets.

Well, almost all. I've used other arguments to create scholarship and grant money out of "thin air," which are beyond the scope of this book.

Appealing and Early Decision

In the last chapter, I mentioned the perils of ED. Because it is binding, you have no leverage to negotiate your award. Yes, there's a "financial out" - but even if you invoke it, you won't have financial aid awards from competing schools to show your top choice college.[30]

Can you improve a financial aid award from a school that accepted you ED? Yes - but in my experience, it's really, really hard. I've had decent results with some colleges (Vanderbilt has been fair to most of my clients, so has Emory almost as frequently), but they are exceptions.

Common sense supports me here too. If you agree that colleges are businesses (gasp!), and businesses want more, not less of your money...

---

[30] Guidance counselors hardly ever explain this to families, out of fear that, if the family rightfully invokes its Financial Out, next year's batch of kids applying to the college in question will be penalized. (At least that's my theory.)

...What is an ED college's incentive to lure you there if you have no other real choices but to accept their offer?

Bottom line - be very careful about applying ED if you need financial aid. If little Ryan or Brandon puts up a fuss, at least ask (strong-arm) them into telling you exactly why their dream school achieved that status.

If you get a good answer (other than, It just felt right the minute I got there!!!), email it to me!

RESOURCE: Our training class on How to Improve a Lousy Financial Aid Offer: www.AppealsClass.com. Includes sample letters and a pre-submission review of your appeal letter.

CHAPTER 32

DO SENIOR YEAR GRADES COUNT?

The short answer: "Yes."

Did you think Junior year was the sole basis for admissions decisions? Many parents do too.

But most competitive college admissions officers say that the first half of Senior Year counts even more than any other part of the transcript.

Why? It is important for applicants to show that they are committed to learning and have pushed themselves by taking challenging classes. An easy course load in Senior Year undermines this positioning.

So if your child loaded up on AP classes in Junior year, but slacked off in his Senior year, that signals to an admissions officer that he is all smoke and mirrors.

"Senioritis" is another, related issue. If you haven't heard warnings yet, you will - there are years and years' worth of crazy stories about top colleges withdrawing their offers of admission in June, after they find out that the top student they thought they were getting flunked three courses and got C's in second half of Senior year.

These stories are rare, but they are fact-based. Don't become one of 'em - make sure you finish up your Senior year strong, instead of limping across the finish line.

CHAPTER 33

LEARNING DISABILITIES - TO DISCLOSE OR NOT TO DISCLOSE?

Parents frequently ask me whether they should tell admissions that there's a learning disability. Should their child indicate on the application that he received resources such as a 504 or IEP to help him during high school?

They wonder if disclosing this issue would hurt their chances of admission, since taking tests untimed and other accommodations might seem like an unfair advantage.

This is a tough question to answer. Plenty of people will disagree with what I have to say.

To me, the only important issue is NOT whether a child will get into a particular school, but will he SUCCEED there and be positioned for success for the next 40+ years.

Many colleges have started to recognize that many students learn differently (which is why I prefer the term "Learning Difference" instead of "Learning Disability.")

Examples abound of super-successful people who would have been classified as Learning Disabled include Einstein, Thomas Edison and Richard Branson (founder of Virgin Records, Virgin Atlantic and a bunch of other companies including Virgin Galactic, a space travel company).

Scores of colleges have implemented programs to help those who learn differently. (Recommended: Peterson's *Colleges for Students with Learning Disabilities or AD/HD*). Some are unstructured, and offer only what the law requires, others are more structured, featuring regular meetings with an advisor and other accommodations.

Some colleges treat their LD kids as special classes, other colleges "mainstream" their LD students so they're indistinguishable from the rest of the student body. Example: Marist College has special software installed on all of its library computers instead of only on certain, designated computer stations. So you avoid issues associated with singling out kids "over there," calling attention to their learning issue by virtue of where they're sitting.

A common theme you'll hear from heads of LD programs at colleges is that the sooner the child learns to self-advocate, the better. In other words, instead of underperforming, the student should seek whatever accommodations or resources are available.

Back to the "Disclose or Not to Disclose" question. If your child learns better with accommodations, I would disclose it to give your child the best chance to succeed in college.

Plans take time to implement - the school needs to recruit and assign tutors or specialists, they must alert professors, they must grant software access - and other items. You can't just show up at a college and say "I need help" and expect a full-blown plan in 15 minutes.

I heard a story from the head of a LD department at a private East Coast college. One day, about a month into first semester, a young woman - a matriculated student - strolled into her office. She told the department head that she was from California, and was interested in hearing about this college's programs for LD kids such as herself.

The department head asked what her learning challenge was.

She was blind!

She didn't disclose this on her application because she was afraid that she wouldn't be admitted. Now, the department head had to scramble to find accommodations for her. This doesn't happen overnight, so the student lost almost half a semester, had the LD accommodations been instituted before classes started.

How to disclose

Not all learning disabilities are equal. One classification that causes a fair amount of skeptical eyebrow raising is ADHD.

Why? For reasons you'd probably suspect: it's commonly known that doctors tend to over-diagnose kids this way, so they can prescribe school performance miracle drugs like Adderall.

I'm not saying that admissions officers perceive ALL ADHD kids as gaming the system. If your child has been classified this way, understand that admissions officers will treat you differently than a child who is deaf, or has documented processing, executive functioning or other issues.

Here's how NOT to disclose a learning disability: by writing an essay that makes a laundry list of excuses for why you underperformed. I would have gotten A's across the board but...

Instead, disclose the learning challenge in the context of how you succeeded despite this issue. How you overcame this obstacle.

One of the most compelling essays I reviewed this year was from a client who told her story about how, since she was in elementary school, she felt stigmatized by being in Resource Room.

So she set the goal of getting out. That meant going to learning specialists after school, taking extra time to study and making other sacrifices when other kids were playing or otherwise having fun.

She even described how her disability prevented her from doing the monkey bars as easily as the other kids, so she would go back to the playground when no one else was around, just to practice.

Then, one day in 6th grade, without warning, she was called into her guidance counselor's office. He told her that she was no longer required to be in Resource Room!

Do you see why this "Hero's Journey" is a better story to tell than a whiny, excuse-laden, defensive tale?

Everyone, including college admissions officers, would rather read about an underdog who persevered and overcame obstacles, compared to a bunch of complaints and excuses from entitled, whiny kids.

From a "40 - not four year" perspective, every potential employer would bet on the candidate who had the drive to claw and scratch her way to success, instead of the privileged kid who never knew adversity and made great grades and had things easy her entire life.

In this way, LD kids have an advantage over the rest of the non-classified population!

CHAPTER 34

DISCIPLINARY INFRACTION?

How you disclose it is more important than the actual "it"

Nobody's perfect, even though it can appear that way on college applications (and Facebook).

What do you do if you've had a major screw-up that resulted in a school or legal disciplinary action? (I'm talking about getting caught cheating, drinking or using drugs, not murdering your neighbor.)

The first thing you should do is take responsibility for whatever happened. Don't blame others for your actions. You can explain the context for your behavior, which may include peer pressure, but be clear that it was your decision to do what you did.

You should also discuss the lesson you learned. This is the most important thing the admissions committee will be searching for, as they try to determine whether you're a wiser person for having gone through this experience or you're a threat to student safety and a potential liability to the college.

Last point: if your infraction involved a court order which resulted in a sealed record, you should not bring it up on your college application. The court seals records because it determines that its current punishment is enough, there's no need for the defendant to pay any further price to society in the future by having the incident known to the public.

CHAPTER 35

NOT-SO HIDDEN DANGERS OF SOCIAL MEDIA

Look, even if I, a parent, teacher or some other "expert" told a kid to voluntarily get off Instagram, Snapchat or whatever the new social media flavor of the month is, he wouldn't. So you won't find that advice here.

But keep in mind that everything you post online, every dumb picture or written entry, will be around for GENERATIONS. Meaning that your kid, your grandchildren and their children, etc. will be able to see the record you've left for posterity.

Think about that next time you post that shot of you doing a shot of Tequila, bare chested and grabbing your crotch.

Colleges were early adaptors of marketing on Facebook and other social media channels, using this medium to create buzz and followers to increase applications submitted.

Admissions officers use social media too. There have been a ton of articles that describe how colleges troll Instagram and other sites to check on their applicants. Each year the percentage of admissions officers admitting to this increases.

You may already know some of the more popular defensive tactics, like adopting a fake name for online purposes. Good move.

Regardless of whether you post under your own name or a Nom d'Instagram, I won't belabor the point:

Don't be a moron - online or off!

If you display moronic behavior, some admissions officer is bound to find out.

Bottom line: before you submit your applications, "audit" your online presence and remove any stuff that does not portray yourself in the best light.[31]

The flip side: if a local publication wrote an article about your accomplishments, but it's not online yet, either ask the publication to post it or get it online yourself (have a friend post it). Nice to have a positive online footprint!

Go on the offensive

Here's another angle on social media: consider creating or beefing up a profile that is admissions-officer-friendly. Hey, if they're going to be spying on you, why not serve up what you want them to see?

Three years ago, I suggested to a client, Alexa, that she create a Linkedin profile.

Predictably, she responded, "Ew, why would I do that?"

My reason was that she was an aspiring business major, and she had participated in several congruent activities since we first started working together, in 10th grade, including internships and paid positions.

Alexa was very happy with her admissions results - she got into Northeastern's business programs, even though her weighted GPA and ACT scores were substantially below those of other kids from her high school who were denied. (I know I said that getting in is never due to One Thing, but this sure felt like the main reason. :)

---

[31] A client, a girl named Jamie, once asked me to do this for her. So I went on her Instagram, scrolling through all of her pictures. After 10 minutes, it started to feel a little creepy, since she had a lot of of photos of her with her friends at Sweet 16s, at the beach, and I was alone in my basement office. Ultimately, I found a photo of her and friends with alcoholic-looking beverages, and reported back to her. That was the last time I agreed to do this.

CHAPTER 36

HOW TO PRY YOURSELF OFF THE WAITLIST

It's a weird letter.

This year's batch of applications was the largest and most qualified ever. Each applicant was gifted, had near perfect grades and SAT scores, hailed from a country you cannot pronounce, cured a deadly disease over the summer and can juggle seven dinner plates while singing our fight song backwards, in German.

So we're not letting you in.

But we're NOT "rejecting" you either!

"Huh?"

Welcome to College Purgatory: the Wait List, or "Deferred Admission."

I won't kid you, it's not easy to escape this neither here nor there status.[32] The odds at many schools are daunting. But you DO have a slim chance. Here are five tips you should follow to help:

1. Tell admissions that you STILL want "in." Admissions officers care about their "Yield," the ratio of admitted (not deferred!) applicants to matriculated students. The higher this ratio, the higher ranked the school. Open a dialogue, try to find out where you fall on the list, if they will tell you. Have your guidance counselor make the call, if you like (if you're too much of a wuss). And if he or you

---

[32] However, this year (2019) it seems like more colleges are dipping into their waitlisted candidates.

can tell your admissions officer in good faith that, if they let you in, you will attend, do so!

2. Update your file with new academic information. Send in any new grades or scores if they will help your cause. (Hint -a "D" in Pop Culture probably won't help.)

3. Update your file with new awards or honors received. Named all-county? Receive "outstanding student" or some other recognition? Send it along.

4. Submit an additional recommendation letter from another teacher, employer, internship supervisor, etc. Not Mommy's or Daddy's alum friend who barely knows your child. Most colleges limit the number of recommendations they'll consider. But hey, you're on the Wait List. You're not in. You have little to lose.

5. Communicate regularly, but do NOT overdo it. Showing you're interested via Steps 1-4 is great. Sending cookies or other gifts is over the top. Camping outside of the admissions office is creepy.

Don't give up! Some kids get off the Waitlist in August!

And bear in mind that colleges like to see grit and determination...

...Especially when combined with a healthy amount of shameless sucking up!

Good luck!

CHAPTER 37

SAT VERSUS ACT

I'm no test prep expert, but let me share some thoughts I've developed over the years.

1. There's no correlation between the price you pay a tutor and your results.

2. Stay away from the Big Boys - Kaplan, Princeton Review, Huntington Learning Center, etc. They tend to hire tutors on the cheap, and push products and programs instead of customizing learning for individual students. (This is an opinion, so don't sue me. And many of my clients have had decent experiences with these companies, so they're not all that bad.)

3. Just because your tutor scored high on the SAT does not mean that he can teach you how to do so. There's a difference between scoring well and teaching well.

4. Just because your tutor went to a snooty college doesn't mean that he's better than a tutor who went to a local college.

5. Every college accepts both the SAT and ACT, so focus on the one that works best for you. (Either take one of each or a hybrid, half-and-half diagnostic exam like we and other test prep companies offer.)

6. Most colleges "super score" the SAT - allow you to pick the highest scores from multiple sittings.

7. Taking a test two-three times is enough. Four or more is obsessive and past the point of diminishing returns, for 98% of test takers.

8. I have mixed feelings about taking the PSAT in Sophomore Year, mostly because kids haven't had all the math covered on the test. Yet, it's good practice from an endurance perspective.

9. About 30% of kids do better on either the SAT or ACT, so take both or a half-and-half diagnostic if you're unsure whether you're in the 30% or 70% category.

10. Tutoring, class instruction and test prep books don't work if the kid doesn't put in the requisite time.

11. I know you're busy, ALL kids are busy.

12. It's not unusual for kids to improve their SAT 300 points or more compared to their PSAT.

13. It is unusual for a kid to score higher than the average ANY of his three practice tests.

14. There are PLENTY of top, respectable, "name brand" colleges who do not require the SAT or ACT. See FairTest.org.

15. The SAT and ACT are NOT going away, though, mostly because they are predictive of a student's ability to perform in college. (No, they're NOT perfect!!!)

16. No one gives a rat's patootie how you did on your SATs for the rest of your life (unless you go into private equity/investment banking, I'm told).

17. High standardized test scores correlate well to college academic performance. Higher correlating factors: whether your parents went to college. Your family's level of affluence. And other "unfair" factors.

18. If you aspire to an Ivy or other super-competitive college, find out from your guidance counselor when the SAT Subject Tests are given. You may need to take two or more.

CHAPTER 38

COLLEGE BOARD: FRIEND OR FOE?

FACT: The College Board is a "non-profit institution of higher education formed in 1900 to "expand access to higher education." It's best known for administering the SAT and its websites, CollegeBoard.org and BigFuture.com publish great information for the college-bound student and their parents.

But there's another (darker?) side to this entity.

Example: Did you know that the College Board also used to be in the lending business?

It was, until it was sued by then-New York Attorneys General Cuomo and Connecticut A.G. Blumenthal.

The charge: Deceptive marketing practices (gasp!)

The states of New York and Connecticut alleged that the College Board failed to disclose that its lending subsidiary was featured prominently on certain college websites.

The College Board settled the charges without admitting or denying the allegations and got out of the lending business.

Example Deux: Ever wonder why, after you register for an SAT, you start hearing from obscure colleges all over the country?

Because the College Board sells student data. This is big business.

To access this data, each college reportedly pays a subscription fee of $15,000.

Then, it's $.70 per name. Member colleges can sort by race, gender, zip code, income and several other "selects" that kids unwittingly share when they register for a College Board name and password.

Northeastern University reportedly sent 200,000 pieces of direct mail in 2018. At $.70 per name plus the subscription fee, that's more than $140,000 to the College Board (and BEFORE printing and postage!).

But they received 60,000 plus applications. Cha-ching!

Harvard reportedly made $2M in application fees in 2011.

I don't know how many colleges have this kind of budget, but if 100 schools spend $100,000 with the College Board on data alone, we're talking real money pretty soon!

SAT registration fees and other nickel and dime charges are merely drops in a very large bucket.

Remember that applying to college is business. Whether or not your child knows it, he or she is in business for themselves, too.

CHAPTER 39

THE "SECRET" ABOUT RANKINGS

Quick, if you had to pick one factor that correlates the most with college rankings in *US News & World Report* - meaning the one thing that predicts how highly a school is rated - what would it be?

Rate of admission?

Quality of education?

Nope.

Answer: endowment per student.

Close second: reputation among peer colleges (comprising 25% of the ranking).

Of course, selectivity is a biggie. And average GPA and SAT/ACT scores of admitted students. So is compensation paid to professors.

Know what you won't find among these factors? Quality of teaching.

US News and World Report publishes its magic formula, which makes it relatively easy for colleges chasing a high ranking to formulate a plan to improve.

Let's take a gander at some of the ways colleges can jigger their rankings.

- Offering free applications. Have you heard of colleges offering free applications, practically begging kids to apply? This expands the pool so they can reject more applicants, increasing their selectivity.

- Beefing up their admissions departments. Colleges spend a ton of money and time soliciting applications (see previous chapter).

- Mining data from affluent zip codes. I mentioned earlier that 1,100 colleges buy lists of students from the College Board (at $.70 per name on top of a $15,000 annual subscription to a software that enables colleges to search by zip code, income level and other "selects." This practice allows colleges to focus on applicants from neighborhoods where it's more likely the families can afford tuition.

- Merit Scholarships. Closely related to the practice of data mining is the strategic offering of merit-based scholarships to affluent families. The concept is that it's OK to offer $10,000 to an affluent family if the college charges $60,000 per year, because it still nets $50,000. So if your grades, scores or other attributes will "class up" the college's profile, you could be the recipient of a fat, juicy scholarship offer!

- Enrollment Management/Marketing Consultants. Colleges didn't come up with these strategies on their own, they hired high ticket consultants to advise them how to grow their endowments and achieve higher rankings. This explains why formerly "joke" colleges (e.g. U Miami, which, in the 80's, you needed a C average, rich parents and a cocaine habit to get in) now requires a top 10% ranking and close to a 2,000 on the SAT. Tulane and Vanderbilt employed the same consultants. In 2005, when the book *College Unranked* (by Lloyd Thacker) was published, the college enrollment/marketing industry was already more than a billion dollar business.

- Cheating. Recently, a spate of colleges admitted that they falsified data about the quality of their admitted students. Emory, Tulane and George Washington University were among the named colleges, but anyone with half a brain in higher education knows that this practice was much more widespread.

The point of this chapter is not to dissuade you or your kids from applying to any "name brand" schools. Certainly, you should weigh prestige as a factor.

But I urge you to look beyond rankings when you assemble your list of colleges.

CONCLUSION

I hope you found the book valuable and you ended up with some valuable "take aways." But understand that this book is only a beginning, because I could not possibly dump out 18-odd years of experience in 100-plus pages.

Final comments: This past week, I spoke to two different clients who, at one point during the past year, had called me with urgent "She's having a nervous breakdown - can you please call?" questions.

Breakdowns aside, each wondered several times along the way whether she'd get into any college.

The results: One client got into Bucknell and Skidmore, where she's going to play Field Hockey.

Client Two got into Harvard, Duke, Williams and several other elite schools.

(They're each feeling better.)

The college process is full of ups and downs, including occasional near nervous breakdowns. It's an intense, uncertain time, so you can't eliminate stress or fear of the unknown.

My best advice is to focus on the 40 year timeline, not merely the next four. And to have a "Plan B," which frequently is better than Plan A.

Thanks for reading this book, please send me your questions, comments, lavish, borderline disturbing praise, info about stray typos and gentle criticism. You can email me at college@lockwoodcollegeprep.com or call the office: 516.882.5464.

SAMPLE COLLEGE TIMELINE

9th Grade

- Meet with guidance counselor. Ask about classes, teachers, standardized test timeframe, college nights (even if typically for upperclassmen.)

- Select the most challenging classes available that you can muster. (Example: target AP classes instead of honors when available)

- Think "CASA"© - Consistent, Atypical, Strategic Activities: look to join clubs, teams, get involved, but don't settle for what everyone else does.

- Summer plans should include an "Atypical Teen Activity" (Internship? "Shadowing?" Special project?) in addition to traditional, goof-off fun stuff.

- Got Naviance (college selection software used by many high schools)? Do the emotional intelligence and career inventories ("Do What You Are" is what it's currently called).

- Division I-caliber athletes, reach out proactively to coaches of schools you're interested in. It's not too early.

10th Grade

- Meet with guidance counselor to update college planning.

- Play around with Naviance, particularly the "emotional intelligence" test ("Do What You Are") and the career exercise. They each take about 25 minutes, don't whine about it! (You'll want to come back to this exercise in a year or so.)

- Consider taking the PSAT (it's offered in October each year, but most kids don't take it until Junior year, when it "counts" for consideration as a National Merit scholar.

- Continue with your CASA© (Consistent, Atypical, Strategic Activities) approach. Remember, quantity of extra-curricular activities is much less important than quality. Don't throw a bunch of [stuff] up against a wall and see what sticks. Strategically speaking, try to hone in on at least one activity that is related to a field you may be interested in majoring in. Example: business majors can intern for a small business, marketing/communications-oriented kids can lock down an internship at a local advertising agency.

- Ask your guidance counselor about Subject Tests. Some competitive colleges "strongly suggest" (read "require") two Subject Tests. Get one under your belt.

- Enroll in the most challenging classes you can handle for next year. The most important factor in admissions decisions is how much you have challenged, or pushed yourself academically. That means loading up with APs instead of honors or regular curriculum classes

- See some colleges - a large, state school, a mid-sized college (3,000-6,000) and a small (about 2,000 kids) when in session, just to get a feel for the scale, the classes, other intangibles that you can't really analyze until you're face to face with 'em.

- Summer: Think "Atypical" or "enrichment" activities. Take a class, even an online "MOOC" (Massive Open Online Classes - offered by several entities like Coursera, EdX and Udacity). But not the whole summer - get some relaxation in too!

- Athletes, performing artists - reach out to coaches/program heads to introduce yourself, open a dialogue.

- Parents: get a handle on the financial aid rules, loopholes and landmines. The financial aid formulas penalize some kinds of savings accounts more than others, some, not at all. Explore financial moves that can enhance your eligibility. See How to Pay "Wholesale" for College and our website, CollegePlanningGuru.com for more information.

11th Grade (The Big Year):

- Get great grades! Kick butt. (You needed a book to tell you this?)

- Make sure you're registered on time for all SAT/ACT tests. Check out http://sat.collegeboard.org/register for the SAT and http://www.act.org/content/act/en/products-and-services/the-act/registration.html for the ACT.

- Participate in meaningful Atypical Teen Activities.

- Give serious consideration to whom you'll ask to write your teacher recommendations.

- Attend your school's "College Night".

- Attend a local College Fair (one is enough!)

- Take at least three college trips (make sure you include small, medium and large schools if you haven't seen examples already)

- Start your personal statement at the end of June, get one draft done in July, turn two more by August and you'll be in great shape before school resumes!

- Finalize your school resume.

- Line up teacher recommendations - the earlier you ask, the more considerate you'll be to your teachers.

- Athletes: proactively reach out to coaches (see Student AthleteWorkshop.com for more details)

- Performing and other artists: research what's required at the colleges you're interested in: music, sample monologues, portfolios, etc.

- Parents: see the 10th grade section tips for college financial planning.

- Parents: for each college on your list, research their financial aid deadlines and what forms they require. Kids - help your parents out!

12th Grade

- Summer: crank out your essays, do the applications. You have time now, you won't have nearly as much once school resumes. (Your workload will make you feel like teachers have no idea that you're dealing with college applications.)

- If you didn't complete your essays before school resumed, do so ASAP before the year is under full swing.

- Visit colleges when in session (to sit in on classes, talk to students, professors)

- Get great grades (were you hoping for advice like "Eh, let your marks slip a l'il bit?")

- Retake SAT/ACT if necessary.

- Submit final list of colleges to guidance counselor, inquire what they need from you to ensure applications sent on time and correctly.

- Make sure the folks you asked to write recommendation letters actually are doing so.

- Correspond with admissions representatives (demonstrate interest).

- Parents: See the college financial planning tips for 10th graders, above. There may be some last minute things you can do to enhance eligibility.

EPILOGUE

I'M STARTING A NEW BUSINESS

I'm a college finance and admissions consultant, but I've thought for a while about going into a new business.

And I want to be partners with you!

Check that, I want you to run the whole thing (what was I thinking? I don't want to do any real work!). Here's the plan:

First, we (you) will "invite" candidates for your services to "apply" to you, paying an application fee of, say 75-100 bucks.

Then you evaluate the candidate, to tell him or her whether they qualify. (Less than 15% meet your standards, by the way.)

The good news for your business is that, thanks to my ingenious marketing plan, you will have tens of thousands of applicants for about 2,500 spots.

When the stars align and you decide that a select few are indeed, a good fit for your services, you then inform them, on a predetermined day (not before - you need to tease them and make them wait), that they have earned the "privilege" of paying you...

...wait for it...

$300,000!

You brace yourself for your customers' outrage, complaints...

Instead, they are delighted!

In fact, your new customers go out and buy merchandise with your logo and brand: sweatshirts, stickers for their cars, pennants for their walls and other indicators that they've "bought in" and joined an exclusive club (cult?), thereby advertising your business for free!

Actually, they're paying YOU for the privilege of advertising your product, if you want to be completely truthful!

One more thing – please note the absence of any rigorous analysis by your prospective customer about the quality of your product – meaning, the benefit you provide to them.

Your customers will assume that, because you accept only a fraction of the potential customers who apply for your services, you must be top notch!

Otherwise, why would your business be in such demand?

I'm sure you've figured out that I'm talking about the college application process, because you seem like one sharp cat (I can tell).

I attempted to make my description sound ridiculous, but I didn't have to try too hard.

To wit:

Higher Education was a $440,000 Billion industry, way back in 2003, according to *College Unranked* by Lloyd Thacker.

That same year, more than 300 entities were registered as Higher Education Marketing companies.

In 2011, the median budget for advertising by colleges was $800,000, according to Lipman Hearne. (Reminder: "median" means that half of the colleges surveyed spent more than 800K!) In 2001, the median was $260,000.

The Huffington Post reported that the Federal government earned a staggering $51 Billion in profits from student loans in 2011.

To put this number in perspective: Exxon, the most profitable company in the U.S., earned $44.9 Billion, Apple earned $41.7 Billion. JP Morgan, Bank of America, Citigroup and Wells Fargo earned $51.9 Billion...combined!

But now you have a leg up on 98% or so of your peer-students and parents, because you're starting to learn the truth.

WANT MORE "LOCKWOOD?"

Pearl and Andy Lockwood created their proprietary "P4" approach to college planning:

Plan: Uncover a child's "wiring," then discover careers and majors where they can make a living and love what they do!

Path: "Back into' a set of colleges reputable across a cluster of suitable majors/careers

Position: Optimize each child's ability to get into his top choice college, as early as 9th grade with strategic and fulfilling extracurricular activities, test prep and culminating with expert editing and advice on the essays and applications

Produce: Going after any and all funding available, including need-based, merit-based and other, creative strategies.

To speak with our team about college advising for your family and our approach, visit www.LockwoodCollegePrep.com/case-studies or call 516.882.5464.

Made in the USA
Middletown, DE
18 February 2022

61299469R00142